MAKING SENSE OF
THE
REVELATION

How You Can Comfortably Read The Revelation of Jesus Christ

Dr. Rod Nielsen

© 2023 by Dr. Rod Nielsen

All rights reserved. No part of this book except for the Appendixes may be reproduced in any form without written permission from the author.

Names and identifying information in this book have been modified to protect the privacy of the individuals involved.

Cover design: Hannah Myers

Cover Images: Samuel Yee, unsplash.com, 2019.

Interior design: Hannah Myers

Interior Images: joopie, freepik.com.

ISBN 979-8-9859111-2-1

All Scripture quotations, unless otherwise indicated, are taken from the Holy Bible, New International Version®, NIV®. Copyright ©1973, 1978, 1984, 2011 by Biblica, Inc.™ Used by permission of Zondervan. All rights reserved worldwide. www.zondervan.com. The "NIV" and "New International Version" are trademarks registered in the United States Patent and Trademark Office by Biblica, Inc.™

Dedication

This book is dedicated to Agape Christian Church of La Porte, IN where I first taught The Revelation. In Bible Study and in Sunday sermons I shared this material with my congregation who patiently listened and gave me feedback on the effectiveness of my teaching, then encouraged me to continue developing and improving the teaching.

Contents

Forward xiii
Introduction xix
Chapter One: 1
The Purpose and Context of the Revelation 1
    The Context of The Revelation 3
Chapter Two: 9
Techniques Used in Writing the Revelation 9
    The Old Testament 9
    Repetition 9
    Recapitulation 10
    Symbols 10
    Typology 14
    Hyperbole 15
    Progressive parallelism 15
Chapter Three: 18
Important Concepts the Reader Must Understand 18
    Heaven 18
    The Kingdom of God 20
    The Millennium 22
    True Israel 26
    The Battle of Armageddon 28
    The Great Tribulation 32
    The Second Coming of Jesus 32
    Life After Death 34
    The Rapture 36
    Judgment 39
    The Anti–Christ 41
Chapter Four 42
The Text of Revelation 42
    Part One: Chapters 1:1–3:22 43
    Part Two: 4:1–8:5 74
    Part Three: 8:6–11:19 81
    Part Four: Ch. 12–14:20 85
    Part Five: 15:1–16:21 90
    Part Six: 17:1–19:21 93
    Part Seven: 20:1–22:21 100
Reader's Study Guide 106
Appendix 108
Bibliography 111

Acknowledgments

I thank my Lord and Savior Jesus Christ who gave His life to cover my sins and called me to preaching/teaching ministry. I thank Him also for giving The Revelation to the Apostle John who passed it to us. And I thank Him for promising to come again.

Secondly, I thank my wonderful wife, Lisa Nielsen, who always encouraged me to study that I might preach and teach honestly and effectively. She supported taking the time necessary to do my research and development of this book. She continually encourages me to find ways to get my forty plus years of study and writing to Christians who will benefit from the words God has given me.

I thank my brothers Dale Nielsen and Andy Nielsen who reviewed and helped in editing the text. I thank Doug Ladika, Danny Stevenson, Rob Hensley, Bill Mc Pherson, Jeremy Floyd, Gary Mc Killip, Doug Taylor, Vern Newman, and Kevin Anderson who listened attentively to the draft of this book and encouraged me to publish. I also thank Hannah Myers who created the cover and formatted the book for publication.

How I long to breathe the air of Heaven
Where pain is gone and mercy fills the streets
To look upon the One who bled to save me
And walk with Him for all eternity

And every prayer, we prayed in desperation
The songs of faith, we sang through doubt and fear
In the end, we'll see that it was worth it
When He returns to wipe away our tears

There will be a day when all will bow before Him
There will be a day when death will be no more
Standing face to face with He who died and rose again
Holy, holy is the Lord

And on that day, we join the resurrection
And stand beside the heroes of the faith
With one voice, a thousand generations
Sing, "Worthy is the lamb who was slain"
"Forever He shall reign"[1]

From Hymn of Heaven by Phil Wickham

---

[1] *Hymn of Heaven*, Phil Wickham, June 25, 2021, Fair Trade Services and Columbia Records

FORWARD

Probably no other book in the Bible confuses Christians more than The Revelation. As a preacher I receive more questions about this book than any other. Bible readers seem to be mystified by The Revelation even if they understand the other 65 books in the Bible. They say "It just doesn't make sense to me." It's not really that difficult to understand. I want to help you grasp the simplicity of the message without getting lost in the details.

The Revelation is NOT about identifying when Jesus is going to return to Earth. It's purpose is not to teach a buildup of events that immediately precede the second coming of Christ so that He can reign on Earth in His kingdom for one thousand years. Rather than predicting monumental events that signal Jesus' return, John's book is intended to encourage and challenge the reader to live for and like Christ in the time between His first and final comings.

When my preaching/teaching ministry began I knew that one day I would teach The Revelation, and I like many was intimidated by it. William Barclay has called it strange, different, and "notoriously difficult for a modern mind to understand."[1] My mind, having been scrambled by The Late Great Planet Earth[2] many years before, I realized that I couldn't teach this book successfully without careful and concentrated study. I struggled with six specific passages in different parts of the book that all seem to indicate the end of life on earth and the beginning of eternal life. I thought the book was supposed to end with the second coming of Christ.

Then the kings of the earth, the princes, the generals, the rich, the mighty, and every slave and every free man hid in caves and among the rocks of the mountains. They called to the mountains and the rocks, "Fall on us and hide us from the face of Him who

---

[1] Barclay, *Revelation Vol 1*, p1
[2] Lindsey, *The Late Great Planet Earth*

sits on the throne and from the wrath of the Lamb! For the great day of their wrath has come, and who can stand?" (6:15–17)

The nations were angry; and your wrath has come. The time has come for judging the dead, and for rewarding your servants the prophets and your saints and those who reverence your name, both small and great, and for destroying those who destroy the earth. (11:18)

I looked, and there before me was a white cloud, and seated on the cloud was one like a son of man with a crown of gold on His head and a sharp sickle in His hand. Then another angel came out of the temple and called in a loud voice to Him who was sitting on the cloud, "Take your sickle and reap, because the time to reap has come, for the harvest of the earth is ripe." So He who was seated on the cloud swung His sickle over the earth, and the earth was harvested. (14:14–16)

The great city split into three parts, and the cities of the nations collapsed. God remembered Babylon the Great and gave her the cup filled with the wine of the fury of His wrath. Every island fled away and the mountains could not be found. From the sky huge hailstones of about a hundred pounds each fell upon men. And they cursed God on account of the plague of hail, because the plague was so terrible. (16:19–21)

I saw heaven standing open and there before me was a white horse, whose rider is called Faithful and True. With justice He judges and makes war. He treads the winepress of the fury of the wrath of God Almighty. On His robe and on His thigh He has this name written: KING OF KINGS AND LORD OF LORDS.

Then I saw the beast and the kings of the earth and their armies gathered together to make war against the rider on the horse and His army. But the beast was captured, and with him the false prophet who had performed the miraculous signs on his behalf. With these signs he had deluded those who had received the mark of the beast and worshiped his image. The two of them were thrown alive into the fiery lake of burning sulfur. The rest of them were killed with the sword that came out of the mouth of the rider on the horse, and all the birds gorged themselves on their flesh. (19:11, 15–16, 19–21)

Then the angel showed me the river of the water of life, as clear as crystal, flowing from the throne of God and of the Lamb down the middle of the great street of the city. On each side of the river stood the tree of life, bearing twelve crops of fruit, yielding its fruit every month. And the leaves of the tree are for the healing of the nations. No longer will there be any curse. The throne of God and of the Lamb will be in the city, and His servants will serve Him. They will see His face, and His name will be on their foreheads. There will be no more night. They will not need the light of a lamp or the light of the sun, for the Lord God will give them light. And they will reign for ever and ever. (22:1–5)

One of my Seminary professors, Dr. Robert Lowery had taught what seemed like a more workable approach to make sense of these texts, which he called progressive parallelism. He recommended a commentary by William Hendriksen, More Than Conquerors,[1] from which he began developing his teaching about progressive parallelism. Rather than having been written in a chronological (sequential) way, he said The Revelation was written in several parallel sections, each moving from Jesus on earth to Jesus returning to take His followers into eternal life.[2]

My research led me to a twelve–part sermon series, Bible Prophecy and End Times by Dr. Jack Cottrell.[3] Cottrell addressed some of the specific issues that I needed to understand in order to properly interpret The Revelation. In 2013 Matt Proctor, President of Ozark Christian College led the North American Christian Convention in a study of The Revelation. Proctor (who also studied under Professor Lowery) produced Victorious, A Devotional Study of Revelation.[4] He presented this simple summary of The Revelation: "Things are bad. Things are going to get worse. We win!" He also invited six preachers to teach the convention through The Revelation from the perspective of The Revelation being a call for the church to remain faithful to Jesus.[5]

Bringing these sources together, along with copious pages of notes taken from reading and classes, it all started to make sense and I was finally able to comfortably read The Revelation. I no

---

[1] Hendriksen, *More Than Conquerors*, Grand Rapids, Baker, 1939
[2] This will be thoroughly explained later.
[3] Cottrell, College Press Publishing, 2006
[4] Proctor, *Revelation*, 2013
[5] Aaron Brockett, Randy Harris, Jon Weese. Kyle Idleman, Rick Atchley, and Proctor.

longer felt that I had to explain specifically who and what every image in John's vision represented. Instead I focused on the idea that this is not as much about the second coming of Christ, even though that is involved in the message, as it is about encouraging Christians of every age to remain faithful to Jesus.

Two ideologies are constantly at war. Thus, every Christian in every age faces three forces under the influence of Satan that challenge our faithfulness to Christ. One is government persecution. From the time of the earliest Christian churches governments have sought to force believers to renounce the Savior in favor of bowing to the government. A second force is cultural seduction. Because cultures cannot accept a different value system, especially a Christian's value system, they try to seduce Jesus followers to reject Jesus' values and accept their cultural norms. Third is false teaching, especially in the church. We see these forces at war with Christ and His church throughout The Revelation. The Revelation is intended to help Christians resist these influences.

Understanding this conflict makes understanding The Revelation easy and takes away the fear of the message for the Christian. For those who do not believe Jesus, The Revelation should scare them into an honest reassessment.

INTRODUCTION

The purpose of apocalyptic Biblical literature is not to predict future events but to interpret current events and circumstances in light of the supernatural world and God's eternal plan. We must be careful that we don't read current events into The Revelation. While it does anticipate specific happenings, it rather describes the tenor of every age wherein the world fights against Jesus. Knowing this will influence how we interpret the text, making it easier to understand. It will make sense.

It is important to realize that The Revelation was not written to non–believers. We hope and pray that the message will affect the un–believing world in a positive way. However, it will really only make sense to those who believe, and it will also challenge the behavior of the audience.

The Revelation is not about identifying when Jesus will return. No one knows that day except the Father. Rather it is about encouraging Christians who face the forces of an evil world that hates Jesus and all who follow Him. Satan seeks to draw believers away from the Savior and uses cunning and scheming. The Revelation is about hope for whoever remains faithful to the end. Through the pen of John, Jesus encourages the reader to live in expectancy and to resist the persecution of His enemies, the lure of the fallen world with its anti–Christian values, and false teaching.

The modern reader should be careful not to get lost in talk about "the last days." We are in the last days now. All time between Jesus first and second coming are "the last days." "The phrase 'the last days' is never used to speak of the time immediately preceding an appearance of Christ."[1]

Reading The Revelation can be challenging but it is worth your time and effort. Letting it speak to you will greatly impact your walk

---
[1] Dr. Lowery charts at least 12 end–times references. Page 39.

with Jesus. This book will help you make sense of the Revelation and you will more comfortably read this wonderful book. However, it is not a typical commentary in that I don't begin with chapter 1:1 and work verse–by–verse through to chapter 22:21. Making sense of The Revelation is like building a house. One doesn't just build a house. You don't start at the top and work down. You must start with a plan. Then you establish a true foundation and begin building in layers: interior and exterior walls, siding, electrical and plumbing, fixtures and wall covering, floor covering, and finally furnishing.

We will build a foundation by first establishing the purpose and context of John's vision and writing, followed by layers, the techniques the writer used (Old Testament references, repetition, recapitulation, use of symbols, typology, hyperbole, and progressive parallelism). Next we'll define certain concepts that are referenced in The Revelation (Heaven, the Kingdom of God, the Millennium, true Israel, the Battle of Armageddon, the great tribulation, the second coming of Christ, life after death, the rapture, and judgment). How we understand these concepts will determine how we read The Revelation. Finally we'll go through the text although still not in a verse–by–verse way. We'll look closely at chapters 1–3 then discuss the various parallel parts.

I am not ignoring Luke 21 and Matthew 24 where Jesus taught specifically about signs of the end of days. That's a different subject than The Revelation. If that interests you I would urge you to do a careful study of those passages.

When some parts of this writing seems like a sermon it is because I am a preacher, and you can't take preaching out of a preacher. Also some of this teaching comes from a series of sermons I preached on The Revelation.

I'll dispense with quoting every Bible verse mentioned and used. Rather I'll often paraphrase unless it is essential to read the text to fully grasp the intent of the speaker/author. Also I'll not use quotation marks around quoted scriptures, rather I will use italics to set them apart. Most scripture quotations are from The New International Version, 1985 edition. Many are my own translation.

I encourage you to read The Revelation like it is a personal letter from Jesus to encourage you as you battle the three forces rallied against Jesus' people, persecution, cultural seduction, and false teaching.

I have included a short study guide at the end. I encourage you to photo copy that page, then use it to help you remember the points that are made in chapters one and two as you read chapter four.

CHAPTER ONE:
THE PURPOSE AND CONTEXT OF THE REVELATION

Before reading any book it is helpful to recognize the purpose and context of the writing. This is especially important for interpreting an ancient writing. Why would Jesus send this vision to John? Why would John write and send it to the churches? If we establish the purpose and context it'll be easier to receive the message correctly. Let's begin with the purpose.

The purpose of The Revelation is not to help us identify when Jesus is coming back. If it was, certainly they would have known and John would have told us. Biblical prophecy is predominantly more about proclamation than prediction.[1] As Rick Atchley wrote, "Revelation was not written to promote speculation but to produce determination."[2] Christians faced serious opposition. Jesus wanted (and still wants) to encourage His followers to remain faithful, thus repeated are a number of times the writer stated something to the effect of, To him who overcomes I will give the right to eat from the tree of life[3] or some variation.

The purpose of The Revelation is to help us know Jesus and that He's coming back, not when He's coming back. God gave this revelation to Jesus who gave it to His angel who gave it to John, and John faithfully passed it on to us. John begins, "The revelation of Jesus Christ, which God gave Him to show His servants what must soon take place. He made it known by sending His angel to His servant John, who testifies to everything he saw, that is, the word of God and the testimony of Jesus Christ. Blessed is the one who reads the words of this prophecy, and blessed are those who hear it and

---

[1] Predictions found in The Revelation are ambiguous enough to apply to any age and circumstance.
[2] Quoted in Proctor, page 5
[3] Rev 2:7

take to heart what is written in it, because the time is near."¹ Note that it did not say the revelation of Jesus return.

The Apostle's teaching, along with providing a powerful picture of Jesus, helps us understand and love Jesus and His church. It challenges us to worship with intensity and a genuine heart. It encourages us to endure suffering in this world knowing that in the end we will receive the glory of Heaven prepared for us. It emboldens us to witness of Jesus with courage. It shows us just how insidious is evil. And it urges us to truly long for Heaven.

Reading the Revelation will help us recognize Jesus so that we worship Him before He returns, and hang in there when it gets tough. We have to make a choice. Who will we worship? There are only two choices, the prince of this world or Jesus.² We are either on Team Jesus or Team Satan. There are no other choices. The Revelation will prepare us for Jesus' return now, before it happens.

This book will guide the reader away from trying to read and interpret The Revelation in a chronological way. It does not begin in chapter one and work straight through history to chapter 22. Many have tried to interpret The Revelation as just such a history–in–advance. That does not and will not work.

According to the people responsible for the web site wecanknow.com "the date of the rapture of believers was to take place on May 21, 2011 and God would destroy this world on October 21, 2011." Their interpretations I believe are faulty because they begin with a faulty foundation. In a 2002 book Clive Campbell, doing some peculiar mathematical gymnastics predicted that "the rapture" will occur in 2023 and Jesus will return in 2030.³

Approaching apocalyptic or end–times prophetic literature as a sequential roster of events has been called calendarizing. Calendarizing is trying to fit the events of John's vision into the world's historical calendar. The calendarizer believes that there is a code to The Revelation that when broken avails the date and time of Jesus' return. Up to this time in history, every calendarizer who has ever predicted a date for the return of Christ, and there have been many, are zero for everything. No one has been right yet. Those who have predicted a date yet to come suggest that they have broken the

---
[1] Rev 1:1–3
[2] John 12:31
[3] Clive Campbell

code or they have new information or a new understanding that locks it in. The Revelation is not about figuring out when Jesus will return. Calendarizing detracts from the most basic idea of the book of Revelation.

In contrast and maybe opposite of the calendarizing is expecting. Expectors understand that end–times apocalyptic prophetic literature is intended to challenge and encourage Christians to live in expectation that Jesus may return at any moment. While calendarizers focus on what they believe is going to happen when Jesus returns, expectors focus on what our lives should be like now in anticipation of His return. The calendarizer is not happy when he is proved wrong. The expector, the one who is "ever ready" is immune to this disappointment. Jesus cannot break an appointment, because He never made one.

The Revelation was written in such a way that any person at any time and in any circumstance can know Jesus. Its message fits any time and any place where Christians live. The world is a tough place full of evil. It's going to get worse. In the end those who follow Jesus will be victorious.

The basic purpose of The Revelation is to encourage and challenge Christians to faithfulness. Then we can also see how the events of today are part of the same history and we face the same challenges as Christians of all ages. John helps us see past the present to what God already knows. He was not providing new realities. He was showing us our experiences in a new light.

THE CONTEXT OF THE REVELATION

Also necessary to correctly understand The Revelation is to know the context in which John wrote. It won't work to use current events to explain John's vision. It must be seen in the context of John's time (late first century AD). Three particular forces were actively challenging the faithfulness of early Christians. These same forces are active in our world today.

One such force is government persecution. Employing persecution, governments attempt to dissuade believers from allegiance to Jesus. Most of the Christian world was under the rule of the Roman Empire which itself was ruled by a brutal and vicious dictator, Domitian (AD 81–96). Domitian was hated as much as any dictator of our modern times. He was so hated that the Roman Senate passed an official proclamation denouncing him. Representations of him on coins or in statues were destroyed.

He reigned only 15 years but in that time managed to kill 20 senators including some from his own family. He also turned his rancor against Christians who refused to worship the emperor or any of the Roman pantheon. Charged with atheism, an act of treason, many were murdered.

Trajan followed Domitian from AD 98 to 117 and continued persecuting Christians. Pliny, a Roman Governor, recognized that this "superstition" was spreading throughout the land because Christians were serious about what they believed, committing themselves to live like Jesus. He wrote to Trajan looking for advice about how to handle Christians who were charged with offenses against Rome. Should he punish all Christians with no accommodation for age? Should he relent for those who renounce faith in Christ, or is it "Once a Christian always a Christian?" Should he allow for those who disassociate themselves with the name of Christ?

The kinds of tortures inflicted on Christians in interrogation were extremely brutal. Some were tortured several times. Those who persisted in Christian faith were brutally and viciously executed. Those who denied Christ and offered worship to the gods, he discharged. Trajan decided that those who are proven guilty should be killed, but whoever denied his faith by worshiping Roman gods should be pardoned.

Believers in Christ were under intense pressure to renounce faith in Jesus in order to save their lives. We see this in the letters to the churches of chapters two and three. In Ephesus the church persevered and endured hardships for Jesus' name. The church in Smyrna was suffering with prison and persecution, presumably the kind that Pliny wrote about. In Pergamum, a man named Antipas was executed.

Christians in America are not often murdered for their faith in Christ,[1] however we regularly are punished for holding to the Word of God over the ways of the world. Barronelle Stutsman of Richland, Washington was forced to pay a fine of $5,000 because she declined to create a special floral arrangement for the same–sex

---

[1] This author knows of no such deaths in America in recent history.

wedding of a long-time friend and client. Anchorage, Alaska officials tried to force Hope Center, a Christian homeless shelter, to shut down unless they would choose to operate according to government terms. High School football coach Joe Kennedy of Bremerton, WA was fired for praying on the field with players who chose to join him. (He has been exonerated.) Atlanta Fire Chief Kelvin Cochran was fired for writing a book for a men's Bible study. Port Wentworth, GA police officer Jacob Kersey was pressured off the department for a social media post that claimed "there's no such thing" as gay marriage. InterVarsity Christian Fellowship was disqualified from the University of Michigan and other colleges because of their Christian beliefs. Christian professors are regularly discriminated against in hiring or given less status positions at universities. Awful hateful things are routinely spoken against Christians without negative repercussions.

This is not unlike the Romans trying to force Christians to bow to Caesar and call him Lord. Using their power and authority governments, including the United States government at most levels, punish Christians who refuse to go along with their values and agendas.

Another force early Christians faced was cultural seduction. According to Jesus and His Apostles, Christians were (and are) expected to be, as John Stott expressed it, a Christian counter-culture.[1] The church and the world have irreconcilable value systems. In his first epistle the Apostle wrote that we shouldn't love the world or the things of the world.[2] Jesus said, "You cannot serve both God and the wealth of this world."[3]

The world seeks to entice Christians to adapt to the culture, to be like the world in values and lifestyle. It pressures followers of Jesus to conform, to compromise, to become complacent from obedience to Christ. Jesus shared some harsh words with churches that chose to go along to get along. Church members in Ephesus had forsaken their first love.[4] In Pergamum and Thyatira they were eating food sacrificed to idols, and committing sexual immorality.[5] In Sardis, they had soiled their clothes in the world.[6] In Laodicea, having

---

[1] Stott, Christian Counter-Culture, p 15
[2] 1 John 2:15f
[3] Matt 6:24
[4] Rev 2:4
[5] Rev 2:14, 20
[6] Rev 3:4

blended in with the world they became lukewarm at best in their faith, seeking hope in wealth.[1]

By seducing the church to relax her faithfulness in order to be comfortable in the world, the enemy has diluted the message of the church and negated the impact of her place in the world. This is true of the church today as a whole and as individual Christians.

One does not have to look very far today to see examples of Christians and churches who have been seduced by culture and have accepted the world's values in place of Christ's values, becoming neither hot nor cold. Christian standards about sexual relationships, charitable giving, unselfish service to others, and work ethic often are not noticeably different from the world. While we celebrate Christian athletes and entertainers who use their platforms to glorify Jesus, many more don't, falling prey to a condition called CSI, "concealable stigmatized identity," meaning they choose to conceal their Christian identity to avoid negative consequences.

Yet a third force working against Christians is false teaching, especially in the church, teaching that often compromises with the world. Christian values cannot co–exist with cultural values and those of other religions, no matter what bumper stickers say.

Jesus spoke directly about false teaching in the church. The church in Ephesus tested those who claim to be apostles but are not and are false.[2] Christians in Pergamum held to the teaching of Balaam, and the Nicolaitans.[3] People of the church in Thyatira tolerated the woman Jezebel.[4]

Peter identified false prophets in the church who introduced destructive heresies, even denying the sovereign Lord.[5] Numerous other New Testament passages warn of false teaching/teachers in the church.[6]

In the words of one online commentator some "have abandoned any fidelity to the Word of God" and "are flapping in the breeze of relativity and futility attempting to scratch the itching ears of the world to stay relevant."

---

[1] Rev 3:15f
[2] Rev 2:2
[3] Rev 2:14f
[4] Rev 2:20
[5] 2 Pet 2:1
[6] Matt 24:4f,11; Acts 20:29f; Gal 1:6–9; Phil 3:2; Col 2:4,8,18,20–23; 2 Thess 2:1–3; 1 Tim 1:3–7, 4:1–3; 2 Tim 3:1–8; 1 John 2:18f, 22f; 2 John 7–11; Jude 3f

Then and now Christians who have not prepared themselves in the knowledge of God and of His Word are often led astray by a slick, charismatic teacher or preacher. It isn't hard to find churches and preachers who are proclaiming false doctrine. I am talking about things more serious than disagreeing about baptism or spiritual gifts or style of music. This is about teaching that denies the Lordship and all-sufficiency of Jesus and the authority of His teaching (including that of the Old Testament and writings of the Apostles).

False teaching within the church was and is harmful to Christians and tends to cause believers to lose sight of Jesus. His example of living and His teaching lose their impact on the lives of believers. They no longer obey Jesus but rather allow culture to determine what is right and wrong, disregarding what He said. They worship Jesus but don't love Him. They are no longer awed by Him. In the words of Matt Proctor, "When you declaw the Lion of Judah, who is to stop you from living however you want? When you no longer see Him in His awesome holiness you are one step away from sin."[1]

Controlling and manipulating these forces arrayed against Jesus' followers, the government, the culture, and the false teachers, is the prince of this world and the enemy of the church, Satan. Under such intense pressure from the scheming deceiver it is important for Jesus' followers to know that God sees what they're going through. William Hendriksen notes that God sees their tears; their prayers are effective; and it matters to God when they are murdered. The Revelation assures them of ultimate victory over evil and that He will avenge their suffering at which time also He will reward their faithfulness with eternal life.[2]

A great war is going on between God and Satan, a war in which Christ will be victorious. He will conquer. The dragon and his agents will be defeated along with all who have chosen to follow (worship) the dragon. It may not look good for the saints right now but in the end they will reign with Christ.

The purpose of The Revelation is not about knowing when Jesus is coming back. Rather it's about helping the reader truly know Jesus and be encouraged to hold on to faith even when getting beat up by culture and society. It's a warning to never underestimate Jesus,

---

[1] Proctor, p. 29
[2] Hendriksen, p. 14

because Jesus is awe inspiring. He embodies words like glory and splendor and majesty and power and brilliance and authority. As one preacher said, He is our Father in Heaven, but He is not our grandfather in Heaven. He is Lord!

Remember, this was written during a time when Rome had declared open season on Christians. Jews as well sought to suppress faith in Jesus from spreading.[1] Christians lost their jobs. Their families were broken up. They were imprisoned, tortured, crucified. In some places in the world today Christians still live in that fear.

Perhaps you experience it. Maybe not the kind of fear and suffering those early Christians endured, but you have crises, a lost job, a lost life, a family conflict, sickness. Maybe someone hates you because you love Jesus. Maybe you wonder how Jesus could let an 18 year old demented boy shoot up an elementary school. How could He allow our government to codify and celebrate the murder of unborn babies? How could He allow a 7.8 earthquake to disrupt and destroy the lives of thousands of people in minutes?

John knew persecution and trouble. Before writing this book John had been abused, imprisoned, and flogged by the authorities because he preached Jesus the Messiah.[2] When this vision was given to John he got it. The Revelation he was given is intended to show us not only that Jesus is a powerful almighty God who will not be managed by us, but that He has already won the great war between Satan and God. And He will one day return to collect His own when He ultimately and finally destroys His enemies.

---

[1] At the time of this writing it is reported that two members of the Israeli Knesset had proposed a law that would make sharing the Christian Gospel in Israel illegal.
[2] Acts 4:3; 5:18, 40

CHAPTER TWO:
TECHNIQUES USED IN WRITING THE REVELATION

In order to correctly interpret The Revelation it's necessary to understand the literary techniques John used. Much more familiar to people of old than to contemporary readers, apocalyptic literature is its own genre. Apocalyptic comes from the Greek word apocalypse meaning unveiling or revealing. The title of the last book of the Bible "The Revelation of Jesus Christ" refers to revealing the truth about who and what Jesus Christ is. Other apocalyptic literature found in the Bible can be seen in parts of Isaiah, Ezekiel, and Daniel. Apocalyptic literature, especially The Revelation, is characterized by certain literary techniques. We will look at some of the techniques John used.

THE OLD TESTAMENT

The Revelation alludes to or references the Old Testament 414 times in 403 verses. Most are not quotes nor are they explained. We will not try to show and explain each of these. However, it is interesting to find them when reading Old Testament prophecy.

REPETITION

Repetition is simply to repeat a word, phrase, or thought, similar to how this book repeats the purpose of The Revelation and the three forces arrayed against Christian faith many times. Consider these examples. A description of Jesus is repeated several times in the first three chapters. The phrase who was, who is, and who is to come is repeated.[1] Jesus saying "I am coming is repeated seven

---
[1] 1:4; 4:8; 7:8

times.¹ The testimony of Jesus " is repeated.² Certain symbolic numbers are repeated often. Behold is repeated no less than 26 times in calling the reader to pay attention to what is being said. There are several series of sevens.

RECAPITULATION

Recapitulation is quite similar to repetition in that ideas and words are repeated. The difference being that recapitulation repeats to summarize and add. We can see this in the visions of the seven seals, seven trumpets, and seven bowls of wrath. Each vision of seven speaks of destructive punishment on part of the earth as a result of sin and leads to judgment. With the seven seals comes power over one fourth of the earth culminating in the final judgment.³ The seven trumpets tell of destruction somewhat more intense, now one third of the earth and again ends with the final judgment.⁴ The seven bowls of wrath describe even more destructiveness on earth until the end is described.⁵ Calendarizers see these as necessarily sequential as if one must follow another. This reads something into the text that is not there.

Repetition and recapitulation are effective tools to reinforce the message. The world is full of evil, but we know that if we stand firm, in the end we win. We tend to remember things we hear often. That is why advertisers run their commercials more than once.

SYMBOLS

John took advantage of symbols that have understood meaning. For example, a reference today to "9–11" carries much more meaning than simply a date on a calendar. Likewise to speak of "March Madness" brings to mind not an angry month but rather college basketball tournaments.

Symbols aren't intended to provide a photograph and they're not the message. They are tools to communicate God's truth. A reader who gets wrapped up in the details will miss the point. John used symbolism to convey great truths. As John wrote, through the

---

[1] 2:5; 16; 3:11; 16:15; 22:7, 12, 20
[2] 1:2, 9; 12:17, 19:10; 20:4
[3] Rev 6:12-17
[4] Rev 11:17–19; 12:9f
[5] Rev 16:17–21

vision God made known what would happen.[1] Made it known uses a word that means to make known through symbols. John had used the same word in his Gospel where he wrote of Jesus saying He would be lifted up from the earth to make known through a symbol how He would soon die.[2] Professor Lowery pointed out that John used the word "like" rather than "is" 72 times, indicating their use as symbols.[3]

In chapter 1:14–16 Jesus is described as having eyes like blazing fire, His feet like bronze glowing in a furnace, out of His mouth came a sharp double–edged sword. Along with His dress, His hair white as snow, His face like the sun shining in all its brilliance. Try drawing a picture of that. The scene of one sitting on a throne in Heaven[4] suggests that He is coming with power and authority and wisdom, and glory. This is further enhanced with the description of Jesus returning on a white horse.[5] A white horse represents victory.

Satan is seen as an enormous red dragon with seven heads and ten horns.[6] He is aided in his evil by a beast coming out of the sea uttering proud words and blasphemies, a beast coming out of the earth, and a woman sitting on a scarlet beast covered with blasphemous names.[7] Those are some ugly tattoos. These symbols aren't intended to portray real specific beings of those descriptions. Rather, their purpose is to give the impression that Satan and his allies are absolute evil. Images such as these, whether good or bad, are not reality but represent reality. We will miss the point if we look for individuals who appear as a dragon, a beast, or a prostitute, and who come in sequential order.

Numbers are especially symbolic in The Revelation. We do the same today. We tell our children something a thousand times. We tell friends we're available to help 24–7–365. Of course we don't mean that there's never a time we're not available, only that we're ready to help if needed just about any time. Jesus did this when He told the disciples that they should forgive seventy times seven times. Does anyone think He intended to communicate that forgiveness can stop at 490 times? Rather than trying to interpret these numbers exactly

---

[1] Rev 1:1
[2] John 12:32f
[3] Lowery p. 106
[4] Rev 4:2f
[5] Rev 19:11ff
[6] Rev 12:3
[7] Rev 13:1, 5; 17:3

we should instead look for what they represent.

Scholars universally agree that numbers in the Apocalypse are used symbolically, communicating more and other than just their numerical value. Seven should cause us to think in terms of complete or total. Seven churches, think of all churches. Seven bowls of wrath, think in terms of all of God's punishment. If seven is complete, three and a half would be less than complete. Evil is perversion of good so its number is broken seven – 6. Also, if seven is complete, six is one short of complete. 666 is threefold short of completeness. 1000 years means a lot of years, probably not 999 plus one. Twelve is the number of the church (12 tribes of Israel, 12 Apostles of the church). 24 combines the tribes and the Apostles (all of God's people, both old Israel and new Israel). 144,000 is 12 twelves and probably should not lead us to believe that 12,000 from each tribe will be saved,[1] especially considering that John saw a great multitude that no one could count[2] who were saved. Four reminds the reader of the four directions (North, South, East, West) indicating totality.

Certain individuals mentioned in The Revelation are also intended as symbols. The dragon mentioned in chapter 12 is clearly Satan.[3] The beast out of the sea, the beast out of earth, and the woman, the great prostitute[4] don't describe actual and specific persons. Rather they look to government persecution, false religious teaching, and cultural seduction. There have been many "beasts" and "prostitutes" throughout history. Babylon probably refers to Rome, the government persecuting Christians at that time. There are many other "Babylons" as well.

Most of us will need guidance from scholars who have studied for many years in order to be confident in our interpretation of symbols. Even then we'll need to have a rubric for measuring the accuracy of our understanding. Certainly it would be helpful if John explained every symbol for us but, as Lowery wrote, it would diminish the beauty of the book.[5] In this I'll borrow extensively from Revelation's Rhapsody to present seven guidelines for understanding symbols.[6]

---

[1] Rev 7:4ff
[2] Rev 7:9
[3] Rev 12:9
[4] Rev 13:1, 11; 17:1
[5] Lowery, p. 112
[6] Lowery, p. 110–115

1. Interpret symbols in their context. How is a symbol used within The Revelation? How is it used in other contemporary writing? Consider the description of the beast in Chapter 13. This is intended to contrast with the Lamb. Compare the Whore and Babylon with the Bride of Christ.[1]
2. Look for a traditional meaning of a symbol. Except for perhaps "Puff the Magic Dragon," dragons have always been considered as evil and dangerous. Dragons are ugly and grotesque.
3. Note if John himself explains a symbol as he does several times.[2]
4. Trying to find a meaning for every symbol can interfere with John's message. Chapters 4&5 are about worship but the reader can get lost looking for a specific meaning for each symbol. The measurements of the New Jerusalem in chapter 21 may distract from the message that God will live among those who are saved. 12,000 stadia equals about 1,400 miles. Imagine a city 1,400 miles wide, 1,400 miles long, and 1,400 miles high. That's a difficult image to comprehend.
5. Look for how a symbol supports the main idea being discussed. God, with the appearance of jasper and carnelian supports His majesty.[3] The specific jewel is of little importance. The foundations of the New Jerusalem decorated with precious stones. Twelve gates made of pearls. A street of pure gold. What does Heaven need with the jewels and a gold street? This is about beauty.
6. Interpret an obscure reference from that which is clear. The angels of the churches in chapters 2&3 are not the local pastors. Angels are angels. Three times John mentions seven spirits before the throne.[4] As seven denotes completeness, the seven spirits represents the fullness of the Holy Spirit and reminds us of God's total or complete sovereignty.
7. Look for what is simple to understand and accept that we cannot understand everything. It would be dishonest and arrogant for anyone to say he knows precisely the meaning of the number of the beast, 666.[5]

Taking the time to understand the symbols can make it easier for us to apply the message to ourselves. The beasts of chapter 13 represent the government (at that time Rome) and anti–Christian

---

[1] Rev 13:17, 21
[2] Rev 1:20, 4:3, 5:8, 7:13f, 12:9, 17:9, 2, 15, 18; 19:8; 20:4–6, 14
[3] Rev 4:3
[4] John 1:4; 4:5; 5:6
[5] Rev 13:18

forces that seek to harass Christians out of their faith. To assign specific beings today with the beasts will lead us away from John's truth about the threat of government persecution, cultural seduction, and false religious teaching. There have been many individuals throughout history that could be seen as such beasts (Roman Emperor Domitian, Pol Pot, Saddam Hussein).

Symbols aren't meant to be like a photograph. They're not the message but tools to communicate the message. Symbols provoke thought and emotions, stimulate thinking, motivate response, and imprint on our minds. Sometimes they irritate us enough that we pursue a deeper look into their meaning. When we read about locusts we don't look for little grasshopper type bugs that happen to have scorpion tales.[1] We think of destruction and trauma. When we read about the dragon we don't look for a fire breathing lizard. We think of Satan. When we read about beasts we don't think about the Disney character. We think about anti–Christian government (Rome).

TYPOLOGY

Yet another literary technique used in The Revelation is typology. Typology is when an author mentions a "type," a person, thing, or event from the past then applies it to a contemporary reality. The seven churches and their ills and deeds are a type. The antitype is a condition churches have experienced throughout history. Ten days of testing[2] are a type. The antitype is the church at Smyrna being tested.[3] Balaam and Barak[4] form a type. The church in Pergamum following false teachers[5] is the antitype. Jezebel[6] is a type. Misleading of Christians in Thyatira[7] is the antitype.

It wasn't necessary to explain each type to those who received the letters. To merely mention the type was enough for the original readers to connect with the author's meaning.

---

[1] Rev 9:3f
[2] Dan 1:12ff
[3] Rev 2:10
[4] Num 22–24
[5] Rev 2:14
[6] 1 Kgs 16–21; 2 Kgs 9
[7] Rev 2:20

HYPERBOLE

Hyperbole as a literary technique is using exaggeration as a figure of speech. We see hyperbole used by Isaiah and other Old Testament prophets to communicate God's message to and against nations.

A large number such as 1000 years is a hyperbolic way to indicate a long or very long time. A great multitude that no one could count suggests that after referencing 144,000 servants of God who had His seal on their foreheads, the actual number of people who are saved is simply beyond numbers.[1]

The dragon is also described in a hyperbolic way.[2] Rather than just call him a dragon the author describes him with seven heads with seven crowns and ten horns. The two beasts are likewise described in a grotesque way.[3] The whore was dressed attractively holding a golden cup she filled with terrible filth.[4] The images created with hyperbole once pictured are hard to forget. They're not intended to give a false image but to make a point or to make a point clear.

PROGRESSIVE PARALLELISM

Extremely important for understanding The Revelation is progressive parallelism, that is writing sections of a message in parallel, each adding to or intensifying the earlier truth. For example, I am a preacher. I'm a retired preacher. I'm a retired preacher and I continue to preach and teach. The first statement is true. The second and third are also true but each adds another fact or "progresses" the truth.

The parallel parts of The Revelation are concurrent, not successive. They cover basically the time from Jesus' first arrival on earth until and including the end of the world with judgment for the evil and eternal reward for the faithful. They offer not a time line but hope for Christians who are resisting government persecution, cultural seduction, and false religious teaching. We see a call to repentance and warning of judgment that intensifies as they

---

[1] Rev 7:9
[2] Rev 12:3
[3] Rev 13:1, 11
[4] Rev 17:4

progress. "John is not laying out a detailed blueprint for events that are to happen before Christ returns a final time."[1]

When we look specifically at the text of The Revelation we'll identify the following seven parts.

1. Chapters 1–3. Jesus is identified and sends letters to seven local churches. Emphasis is on Jesus coming to claim His kingdom. The churches are warned to hold securely to faith in Jesus Christ until the end.
2. Chapter 4:1–8:5 begins with worship but moves on to describe terrible evil in the world. The end of the world is seen in 6:12–17.
3. Chapter 8:6–11:19 continues to describe evil in the world with ugly descriptors including punishment for sin. The end of the world is found in 11:17–19.
4. In chapters 12–14:20 we read about two ideologies at war. We meet the enemies of God and His servants (Team Satan), namely the dragon, two beasts, and the whore (government, culture, and anti–Christian religion). The enemies are judged and destroyed. We read about the end of the world in 14:9–20 then again in 16:17–21.
5. 15:1–16:21 describes seven bowls of the wrath God pours out on evil in the world, ending with 16:15–21.
6. Chapters 17:1–19:21 emphasize the total destruction of Satan and his agents. Currently they're making war against the Lamb. Eventually the enemies of God are judged and destroyed in 19:11–21.
7. Chapter 20:1–22:21 describes the final judgment on evil and reward for the faithful.[2] The new heaven and new earth are described with beautiful and majestic imagery. This is a final call to obedience and faithfulness because Jesus is coming with reward and punishment.[3]

Rather than being a chronological story, The Revelation is a series of parallel visions intensifying as they go, bringing the reader to the end of the world several times. The repetitive structure makes it easier to understand why the same ideas show up again and again in different ways. As we said above, they tell this basic story. The world is a tough place full of evil. It is going to get worse. In the end those who follow Jesus will be victorious!

---

[1] Lowery, p. 124
[2] Rev 21:7f
[3] Rev 22:7, 12,20

Before moving on let's consider just a few words to answer the question, "Do you interpret The Revelation literally?" Our word literal comes from the Latin littera. A dictionary definition of literal is "according to the letter, or adhering to fact or usual meaning."[1] I submit that literal means to find the intended meaning of the original author, taking into account the context and the grammar, as well as the use of symbols and metaphors, etc. Bruce Metzger's words explain this well. "The book of revelation is unique in appealing primarily to our imagination – not, however, a freewheeling imagination, but a disciplined imagination. This book contains a series of word pictures, as though a number of slides were being shown upon a great screen. As we watch we allow ourselves to be carried along by impressions created by these pictures. Many of the details of the pictures are intended to contribute to the total impression, and are not to be isolated and interpreted with wooden literalism."[2]

The Revelation uses imagery, sometimes graphic and grotesque, to communicate the reality of a war between Team Jesus and Team Satan. It's like we're watching a fantasy movie in which we allow ourselves to be moved by what we see. The specific details shouldn't be separated and interpreted. Rather they should help us understand the whole message.

---

[1] Webster's New Ideal Dictionary, Springfield, MA, G. & C. Merriam Company, 1973
[2] Bruce Metzger, Breaking the Code: Understanding the Book of Revelation, Nashville: Abingdon, 1993. Cited in Lowery note 4 page 164

CHAPTER THREE:
IMPORTANT CONCEPTS THE READER MUST UNDERSTAND

I have found that understanding certain concepts will enhance your understanding of The Revelation. If we keep these ideas in our minds we'll more readily grasp John's message.

HEAVEN

There is one Hebrew and one Greek word usually translated Heaven. They're basically equivalent to each other, and like so many English words, do not always mean the same thing. They're used four ways leading to four ideas of heaven.

One is the divine Heaven. This refers to God Himself. His presence. When Jesus fed 5000 men plus women and children, He looked up to Heaven as He prayed.[1] He was looking to God. When the Prodigal Son said to his father "I have sinned against you and Heaven[2] he wasn't thinking of sin against a place. He sinned against the person of God. David said it was the God of Heaven who gave him his authority.[3]

These references aren't about physical up and down. They're about that which is exalted. The idea of God being high above is not in the sense that He is up there and we are down here but about God being exalted. That's why people bow before royalty and call him/her Your Highness, because height is a symbol of glory and honor.

The idea behind Paul's statement about Jesus having descended from and ascended to Heaven is not about moving from a high up place to a lower elevation.[4] It's about moving from being exalted to

---

[1] Matt 14:19
[2] Luke 15:18
[3] 2 Chr 36:32
[4] Eph 4:9

being one of the guys. It's hard for us to not think in terms of our three dimensions, forward and back, right and left, up and down, but this is different. Is this not where we go when we die? No. We can't. We don't become God. According to the Apostle Paul God alone is immortal.[1]

A second use of heaven refers to the sky above earth. This is about the physical universe measured with our dimensions. The heavens are everything from earth to the farthest reaches of outer space. The Bible tells us that when Jesus comes back He will appear in the physical heavens.[2] This also is not where we go when we die? We can go there now. We can go as high and as far as physical constraints allow.

Thirdly there is the angelic Heaven, the created world of the angels. This Heaven is a heaven of spiritual dimension where we will be like angels.[3] At Jesus' resurrection an angel came from Heaven to roll the stone away.[4] This is the place Jesus left when He came to Earth the first time, and this is from where He will return.[5] This is where we go when we die, but it's not our final destination, and it's not purgatory. There's a time lapse between when some people die and the promised eternal life but it's not clear that they're aware of this time lapse.[6]

In the movie Air Force One, terrorists take over the President's 747. Eventually the President has to abandon the plane and is rescued by an Air Force C-17. When they get him on board they report, "We're changing our call sign. We are now Air Force One." Whenever the president is on board, the craft is Air Force One or Marine One, etc. So it is with the presence of God. When God is present, in this sense, it's Heaven. But this one is only temporary. When Jesus returns and closes the deal, we'll enjoy the fourth Heaven, eternal Heaven.

We will be there one day, in the presence of God, along with the angels and other created beings. This eternal Heaven doesn't exist

---

[1] 1 Tim 6:16
[2] Matt 24:30f
[3] Matt 22:30
[4] Matt 28:2
[5] 1 Thess 4:16
[6] Rev 6:9f may suggest that there is such awareness. The scene is the throne room of God so these souls experience His presence, but there's something yet to come, something far greater and permanent. This may be what Paul meant when he wrote of being absent from the body and at home with Jesus (2 Cor 5:8).

right now. There will be a new Heaven and a new earth.[1] According to Peter the earth will be burned up and God will replace it with a new earth and a new eternal Heaven.[2]

John saw this new Heaven and described it in his writing.[3] This is God's promise for all who are made righteous by believing in Jesus Christ. It's heaven because God will be present with us on this new earth just as He now is with the angels in their Heaven. This is what Revelation leads to. This is the Heaven we will enjoy for eternity. So impressed was Peter by this promise that he challenged believers, knowing that this Heaven coming after this world is destroyed, asking "How should we then live?"[4] What should we do or not do because Jesus is coming back? In the face of government persecution, cultural seduction, and false religious teaching, should we not remain faithful? Shouldn't we stop living for the here and now and set our hearts on eternal Heaven?[5] Without the hope of Heaven we may succumb to persecution, cultural seduction, and false teaching.

THE KINGDOM OF GOD

Kingdom of God or Kingdom of Heaven or the like is used 145 times in the New Testament. This matters to us today because the message of most of Old Testament prophecy, and of apocalyptic prophecy, and of New Testament prophecy is a message of hope, God will send a king who will rule over His people forever.[6] It's a message of hope because being the people of God is rather unpopular. There are always people who want to hurt us. This new and great and good king is Jesus, the one who has been born King of the Jews.

Jesus came to set up His kingdom which He did. He established His kingdom when He came the first time. Interpreters who suggest that the Kingdom of God does not arrive until a future unknown date are saying that Jesus did not do what He said He did. This is essential for understanding The Revelation correctly. The prophecies about the Kingdom of God were fulfilled in Jesus. Both John the

---

[1] 2 Pet 3:13
[2] 2 Pet 3:3-7, 10,121–13
[3] Rev 21:1–4
[4] 2 Pet 3:11
[5] Col 3:2
[6] Isa 9:6-7; Dan 2:44, 7:13f

Baptist and Jesus proclaim that the Kingdom of God/heaven is near.[1] That the Kingdom of God is "near" doesn't mean close. It means that it is starting with Jesus

Once after Jesus had cast a demon out of a man, the super religious guys of that day accused Jesus of using the power of Satan to do this trick. Jesus brilliant response was that this miracle was about prophecy and God's promise. He said since He drives out demons by the Spirit of God it means that the prophecies about this new king have arrived.[2] In a debate with the Pharisees, Jesus said that the Kingdom of God is within His followers.[3]

What is this Kingdom of God Jesus referred to? It's us. It's the church. It's every believer who puts his or her trust in Jesus for salvation. God rescued us from darkness and brought us into the kingdom of the Son He loves.[4]

The Revelation is not intended to predict an earthly kingdom. People who speak of the Kingdom of God as an earthly kingdom probably don't realize that they are saying Jesus failed, that He didn't establish His kingdom the first time. Jesus didn't simply settle for the church and later He'll set up His real kingdom in the millennium. He has already set up His kingdom. The Kingdom of God has come! Not the Kingdom of God will come. Prophecies about the coming of the Kingdom of God have already been fulfilled in Jesus.

Maybe the reason people continue to look for a new Kingdom of God to come is because there's so little evidence that it exists right now. The church looks too much like the world. We don't seek to obey Jesus in all things. We don't teach our children to obey Him in all things. This isn't the result of failure to establish His kingdom. It's the result of lukewarm faith.

The Revelation wasn't written to let us know that the time for the Kingdom of God is near so we can change. It was written so that those of us who are part of the Kingdom of God, striving to live like Christ, will be encouraged to keep going, knowing that the victory has already been won, and Jesus will come back and make all things right. There's also a message for those who reject Jesus or have not yet recognized His Kingdom. I am coming back, and when

---

[1] Matt 3:1; Mark 1:15.
[2] Matt 12:28
[3] Luke 17:21
[4] Col 1:13

I do it will be too late to change your mind. Decide now! Jesus established the Kingdom of God when He came the first time.

THE MILLENNIUM

Many interpreters, I believe, get the millennium wrong because they treat The Revelation as prediction rather than warning and encouragement. They fail to recognize the use of symbols. They see it as a way to know when the last days are here and Jesus is about to come back, rather than its real intent to encourage, challenge, and strengthen us to remain faithful whatever happens. If the best religious scholars of His day failed to recognize the Messiah's first coming, we can expect that scholars today also do so.

We mustn't miss something very important. The Christians of the New Testament period expected Jesus to return during their lifetime. They didn't think this stuff was about 2023. They thought they would witness everything, and it all made sense to them. To read about Russia or China would not have made sense to them. Nor would 24 hour TV news. They believed they were living in the last days. Nowhere in the Bible does anyone answer the question, "Are we in the last days?" because they didn't ask that question. They knew they were in the last days, however long they lasted, and they understood that they were already experiencing much of the end times stuff.

The only place in the Bible where the millennium is actually mentioned is Revelation 20. "I saw an angel coming down out of heaven, having the key to the Abyss and holding in his hand a great chain. He seized the dragon, that ancient serpent, who is the devil, or Satan, and bound him for a thousand years."[1]

The first problem for many readers of The Revelation is that they see "The Millennium" as a title for a specific event, a one thousand year rule of Christ on Earth. It's not a title. It's a description. Hal Lindsey in The Late Great Planet Earth,[2] the Left Behind of an earlier generation wrote, "If you interpret prophecy literally[3] it does teach that Christ will set up a literal kingdom in time which will last in history a thousand years and then go into an eternal form which will never be destroyed." He goes on to describe an

---
[1] Rev 20:1–6
[2] Lindsey
[3] I wrote about what it means to take The Revelation literally at the end of chapter two.

Earthly kingdom with Jerusalem as the spiritual center of the world that all people will come to annually to worship Jesus. This kingdom will be characterized by peace and equality, and by universal spirituality and knowledge of the Lord. I have some real difficulties with Lindsey's interpretation. I believe he combines descriptions of heaven, where there is no more sin and its consequences, with the Kingdom of God. He also seems to think that Jesus failed to set up His Kingdom.

People often ask, Are you pre–millennial, post–millennial, or a–millennial? They mean, do I believe the millennium (probably as described by Lindsay) comes before or after the second coming or do I believe in it at all? I'm pro–millennial. I believe there is a millennium and it's now. The Kingdom of God has already come. Jesus established His kingdom when He came the first time. The prophecies about Christ's rule on earth are not about a physical kingdom. They're about the church. We are the Kingdom of God.

So what is the millennium mentioned in Revelation 20? The word millennium is a Latin word meaning 1000 years. As I said, this is the only place in the Bible that mentions it. A thousand years is a symbol for a long, long time. It doesn't mean ten centuries. In the movie Dumb and Dumber, when Mary told Lloyd Christmas his chance of dating her were "one in a million," she clearly meant "no chance." The millennium mentioned in Revelation 20 doesn't mean 999 + 1 years. It means a very long time. People get messed up because they think that The Revelation is written in chronological order and this millennium happens at the end of history because it comes near the end of The Revelation. Remember, The Revelation doesn't start at the beginning and move straight through to the end. It's a series of trips through history from the first coming of Jesus to His second coming. The millennium comes at the beginning of one of those parallel histories. The millennium began when Jesus came the first time and lasts until He comes the second time. Revelation 20 is not about a new yet–to–come 1000 year period of peace and prosperity. It's about the blessings that come with being part of the Kingdom of God. A look at three promised blessings that we experience now will help clarify this issue.

The first is that Satan is bound. Remember, this is a vision of what happened when Jesus came the first time, not a prediction of something that is going to happen someday. John told us that is why

Jesus appeared as a man.[1] It was written of Jesus that He shared in human flesh and blood so that He could defeat Satan through His death and resurrection.[2] Satan thought he had usurped God's role as king of this earth. Jesus came to show him that he didn't. Was He unable to defeat Satan? He came to take Satan's power away. He did not fail! He did what He promised! Satan was bound.

In an event referred to earlier when Jesus was in debate with some Pharisees who said He exorcised demons by the power of Satan, Jesus said He did it by the power of God, and if He did it by the power of God it meant that the kingdom of God has come.[3] Jesus asked how can someone break into a man's house and steal his possessions unless he first ties up the strong man. Only then could he rob his house. When Jesus came the first time He tied up the strong man and robbed his house. When He gave His life on the cross as a sacrifice for our sins He bound Satan and plundered his power. At His resurrection He put the key in the lock and locked it.[4] Satan no longer has power over us. We're free. I know people think that if Satan is bound, life on earth should be paradise. But that's not what it says. It says that he can no longer deceive us.

Prior to Jesus' first coming the whole earth was under the control of Satan. The battle between righteousness (Team Jesus) and evil (Team Satan) was on. Except for Israel to whom God chose to reveal Himself, every nation, every person was pagan. But now every nation, every person can be free. When Jesus appeared to Saul (Paul) He appointed him as a witness to show people the power of God over Satan.[5] Whenever the Gospel is preached the Devil's house is plundered and people are set free. Satan is bound. Now he's like a snarling dog on a leash. He makes a lot of noise and threats, but he can't do anything to us, unless we give him permission. Do not let your imagination or that of anyone else define what "bound" means. Let the Bible tell you. It means that Satan is defeated. That is the first blessing of the millennium.

I didn't miss the part about Satan being set free for a short time.[6] This doesn't mean that Jesus' life, death, and resurrection failed to handle Satan. It's an arbitrary symbol for Satan's last stand. He will

---

[1] 1 John 3:8
[2] Heb 2:14
[3] Matt 12:28
[4] Rev 1:18
[5] Acts 26:16–18
[6] Rev 20:3; 7f

not give up easily.[1] The millennium began when Jesus came and Satan was bound. It ends when Satan is thrown into the lake of fire.

The second blessing we experience now is that we enjoy the first resurrection.

Two kinds of people are mentioned here.[2] There are those who belong to the beast (Team Satan) and those who belong to the lamb (Team Jesus). People are either saved or lost. There's no other team. Of those who belong to the lamb, there's no distinction between the living and the dead. We're all living. This is the first resurrection.[3] The text doesn't tell us how God brings the dead to life so they can reign with Jesus during the millennium, only that He does. Jesus said if a believer's body dies, he himself will live and never die.[4] Before Jesus, we were dead in sin even though we lived.[5] In Christ we have resurrection. We're alive!

John had already taught of two kinds of resurrection in his Gospel.[6] The first comes to whoever hears and believes God. The second resurrection comes at the parousia[7] to everyone to eternal life, whether dead or alive. Those who don't believe Jesus miss the second resurrection. They instead experience the second death.[8]

The third blessing we experience is that we reign with Christ now. Right now Jesus reigns over His spiritual kingdom, the church. He made us to reign with Him on earth as priests.[9] To reign with Christ means three things. It means that we have power to reign over sin.[10] It means we have power to reign over death.[11] It also means that we have power to reign over Satan in our individual lives.[12] The only way Satan can deceive us and lead us into sin is if we let him. We reign over him.

---

[1] This may well be what Jesus was speaking of in John 14:30, "I will not speak with you much longer, for the prince of this world is coming."

[2] Rev 20:4–6

[3] Rom 6:11; 1 Cor 15:22; Eph 2:4f.

[4] John 11:25f

[5] Eph 2:1

[6] John 5:24–29

[7] Parousia refers to the moment of the second coming of Christ. It is used 24 times in the New Testament however not in The Revelation.

[8] John 5:25, 28f

[9] Rev 5:10

[10] Rom 6:11–14

[11] Heb 2:14f

[12] 1 John 4:4; Rom 16:20

God does promise a future paradise in which we will live in peace and love, where there is no selfishness or hatred, no pain or tears. Sin will no longer be part of the equation of our lives. But that comes later when we go into eternity. How exactly God intends to carry this out isn't important because, however it goes down, we're going to like it.

The three blessings available to us now help us avoid becoming pessi-millennial. Satan attacks but is bound. We have the first resurrection, and we reign over sin and death and Satan.

TRUE ISRAEL

Often when discussing the place of the Jews in the[1] scheme of apocalyptic history people suggest that Israel will return to God and accept Jesus as the Messiah and thus have a special place in God's kingdom. People usually cite Paul in the book of Romans, "I do not want you to be ignorant of this mystery, brothers, so that you may not be conceited: Israel has experienced a hardening in part until the full number of the Gentiles has come in. And so all Israel will be saved."[2] Having studied this carefully I am convinced I can make an argument from these verses that this refers to the physical nation of Israel, and I can make an argument that it refers to spiritual Israel. I could do either with proper exegesis. That tells me that these verses don't provide enough information by themselves to establish with certainty who are "all Israel". We must look elsewhere.

The phrase "all Israel" is sometimes used in the Old Testament to mean physical Israel. There's also reference to "all Israel" in the Mishnah (the written version of the oral traditions defining what the Old Testament means). "All Israel has a share in the world to come. That is then followed by a list of Jews who have no share in the world to come."[3] All Israel then includes and excludes some of physical Israel.

Specific prophecies about Israel are often used in end–times interpretation.[4] Don't assume these are all about physical Israel. I believe that generally, when Israel is mentioned in end–times prophecy, it refers to spiritual Israel, those who trust God and

---

[1] 1 Sam 12:1; 2 Chr 12:1; Dan 9:11
[2] Rom 11:25f
[3] Sanh 10:1
[4] Gen 12:7; Deut 28:63f, 30:3–5; Jer 31:31–33; Isa 2:2f

believe that Jesus is the Messiah, and who are the kingdom of God.

Paul recognized this distinction when he wrote that not everyone who is of Jewish blood is Israel.[1] Writing to Gentiles who place faith in Christ he says that some who are descendants of Abraham are not Israel while believers in Jesus are children of promise.[2] He calls them, Israel. Those born of Jewish descent are physical Israel, and those who believe in Jesus are spiritual Israel.

All the prophecies concerning physical Israel have already been fulfilled. When Jesus came, God retired physical Israel. The book of Hebrews begins by telling us that the Old Testament system ended with Jesus' first coming. Formerly God spoke through prophets but now we're in the last days and He speaks through His Son.[3] God chose Abraham because he believed. He created physical Israel through him. But they proved unfaithful and disobedient so God let them go the way of sin and chose all people who believe and obey, as Abraham did, to be His children. It's striking that God makes no distinction between believers who were born physical Jews and Gentile believers who were not. All believers who call on Jesus' name will be saved.[4] James, the brother of Jesus and leader of the church in Jerusalem said that prophecy about being saved through faith applies to the non–Jews who believe in Jesus.[5]

The New Testament declares that God's promises are extended to non–Jews and that non–believing Jews are excluded. The people of God are those who believe Him, not necessarily those born physical descendants of Abraham. It would seem inconsistent to suggest that now at the end of the book, the authors would suddenly revert to focusing on physical Israel instead of spiritual Israel. The new covenant is with spiritual Israel, not physical Israel.

This is probably the most controversial thing I am going to write about this. Does God have plans for the physical nation Israel to play an important role in the end times? No! The nation of Israel is no more important than Peru or Norway or Andorra. Does God have plans for Jews? Yes, for believing Jews. Otherwise they're just like any other non–believers. No one is saved by the Law, not even someone born with pure Jewish genes. The plan of salvation is the same for

---

[1] Rom 9:6
[2] Gal 4:28
[3] Heb 11:1f
[4] Rom 10:12f; Gal 3:28; Col 3:11
[5] Acts 15:14–18

them as it is for you and me. It's by believing Jesus that anyone may become a part of spiritual Israel, the true people of God, the church, the Kingdom of God. Nobody has birthright into the Kingdom of Heaven. There are two kinds of people, those who have faith in Christ (Team Jesus) and those who do not (Team Satan). Those who have faith are true Israel, the children of promise.

THE BATTLE OF ARMAGEDDON

I'm often asked about the Battle of Armageddon. What is it? It sounds like a war with millions of soldiers from many countries converging on Israel in a decisive battle. It is first mentioned in Joel 3 as part of the Day of Judgment. Armageddon as the location of this great battle is only mentioned one time in the Bible.[1] The name means the Mountains of Megiddo in Hebrew. In Greek in The Revelation and in the LXX it is Armageddon.[2] This is the valley of Esdraelon where Ahaziah the King of Judah was killed by Jehu.[3] This is where Neco of Egypt killed Josiah.[4] This is where Israel gained a victory over the Canaanites as recorded in the Song of Deborah.[5]

The battle itself is mentioned in Revelation 20:7–10. John makes reference to Gog and Magog from Ezekiel 38. Ezekiel prophesied against Assyria offering a word of hope and comfort to Israel in exile. John used this imagery because it was indelibly written on the hearts of Jewish people. Ezekiel was not writing about the second coming of Jesus. Unfortunately, some teachers take the stuff from Ezekiel and Daniel and wrap it around Rev 20 coming up with a fantastic scenario of a great battle such as this:

Israel returns to their homeland and rebuilds the Temple. Because the historic site is currently occupied by a Muslim mosque, it results in war. The ancient Roman Empire is revived. (Somehow it was determined that the European Union is this revival of Rome.) The leader of this new Rome is the Antichrist and he makes a peace treaty with Israel. Peace lasts for 3 1/2 years. Then the Antichrist takes off his mask and reveals himself. He breaks the treaty with

---

[1] Rev 16:12–16
[2] Since Greek has no consonant for H a rough breathing mark was used making the A sound like H. That's why sometimes you find it called Harmageddon.
[3] 2 Kgs 9:27
[4] 2 Kgs 23:29
[5] Judg 5

Israel and invades, sets himself up in the Temple and calls himself God. The king of the south (Africa) and the king of the north (Russia) both invade Israel. God intervenes and destroys both armies. World War 3 breaks out with 200 million Chinese soldiers invading Israel. The Antichrist raises a European army to invade. The Chinese and the Europeans meet in a place called Armageddon. Just as Israel is about to be destroyed, Jesus returns. He lands on Mt. Olivet and rescues Jews and destroys all enemies. Then the millennium begins.

While this is very creative, it's not what the Bible says. We've already seen that the Bible teaches that the millennium is right now, all the time between Jesus' first and second comings. There is a war but it's not a physical war with armies and generals and tanks and jet fighters and massive explosions, and this war is going on already. Remember, this is a vision about the conflict between Team Jesus and Team Satan. This description of the end of the millennium is Satan's last stand.

I witness something similar every spring as a pair of bluebirds vie with house sparrows for a nesting box I provide. The bluebirds claim it and build their nest preparing to raise a brood. The sparrows contest their ownership thus the bluebirds must remain vigilant to keep them out. So it is for mankind. God gave us this beautiful home but Satan wants to claim it (and us) as his. There is a constant battle between him and God. John wrote that Satan, who was bound when Jesus came the first time, would be loosed for a short time.[1] No one knows how long a "short time" is. I don't know why God would allow him to return to deceiving anyone. Maybe He intends to separate truly faithful believers from those who are only playing religion. Whatever the reason, throughout the history of the church Satan has not been allowed to deceive like he did before Jesus came. So during this time of being loosed, the great battle becomes an intensely spiritual battle. It's not military. It's not physical. It's not focused on the land of Israel. It's a worldwide spiritual war against everyone who loves Jesus (true Israel), and involves everyone who is an enemy of Jesus and of His Word.

The war will intensify as the time approaches for Jesus to return, and that's what gets many believers riled. Paul was clear that as we approach the end some Christians will depart from faith in Christ to

---

[1] Rev 20:3

follow deceiving spirits (government, culture, and false teachers).[1] He also wrote of terrible days in which people love themselves and worldly things instead of Jesus. Their behavior will be abhorrent, sometimes religious but not godly.[2] One more thought from Paul, those who choose to follow Christ will be persecuted while evil will get worse.[3] We are in this battle right now. It's very serious and will only get worse. Anti–Christian ideas will multiply and intensify. People will spread lies about Jesus and the Word of God.

There are three important aspects about this great battle that we should keep in mind. First, it's a battle for our minds, a battle of truth. Satan will try harder and harder to deceive people. He'll attack with lies, with false doctrine, and with clever sounding teachings that focus on one part of what Jesus taught while disregarding the call to repentance and obedience.[4] That's why it's ever so important for Christians to be good Bible students. You can't be led astray if you know the truth. But if you have only a superficial knowledge of God's Word, you're ripe for picking by the deceiver. John declared that whoever denies that Jesus is the Christ is the antichrist.[5] Anyone who diminishes the absolute truth of Jesus and what He taught is an antichrist and a deceiver. Satan is fighting for our minds. If he can win us over in what we think and believe, he owns us.

Second, it's a battle for our wills, a battle of wickedness. Satan wants to lead us into sin. He wants to overcome our desire to do what is right. He wants us to give in to society, to the world. He tempts us in new and creative ways. Christians are led to question God. How can anyone deny and disparage the love two men have for each other? How can anyone be so bigoted to suggest that a good man who happens to be a true and faithful Muslim is lost? Suppose a man teaches total love, even if he denies that Jesus is the only way to salvation. How can anyone think that man is deceived and a deceiver? The point is, Satan is fighting for our wills. He wants us to get along with culture rather than stand for God's truth. If he can get us to compromise to him in any way, he has led us away from Jesus.

Third, it's a battle for our lives, a battle of persecution. In many places in our world being Christian is a death sentence. In America

---

[1] 1 Tim 4:1
[2] 2 Tim 3:1–5
[3] 1 Tim 3:12f
[4] How often have you heard that Jesus is all about love to excuse tolerating sin?
[5] 1 John 2:18, 21f

we're not now facing that kind of persecution but it will come. We're already branded as extremists. Soon we'll be outlaws if we stand for truth. This isn't just a culture war, it's the scheme of Satan himself. It's part of his great battle plan against God. These battles aren't against physical Israel. They're against spiritual Israel, the kingdom of God, the church. They're against everyone who believes in Jesus. They are against us!

Paul wrote, Don't let anyone deceive you in any way, for that day will not come until the rebellion occurs and the man of lawlessness is revealed, the man doomed to destruction. He will oppose and will exalt himself over everything that is called God or is worshiped, so that he sets himself up in God's temple, proclaiming himself to be God."[1] There will be a rebellion. People will turn away from Jesus, setting themselves up in opposition to Him. What he called "the" rebellion (not "a" rebellion), is people rejecting Jesus.

There is in this the mention of the man of lawlessness, the man doomed to destruction, literally the son of destruction.[2] I'm not smart enough to identify who this guy is or even if he is a person. If it is a specific person it goes against the rest of the text for the text speaks in a more general way. So I suggest that it refers to anyone who tries to teach a way to salvation that does not include Jesus Christ.

Here is how I understand this. As we near the second coming of Jesus, the two sides of the great battle, Team Jesus and Team Satan, will be polarized and Satan will be clear as the anti–God. Paul said in verse 6 that the man of lawlessness is being held back or bound. He will be let loose for a time and the Lord Jesus will overthrow him. The end–times scenario includes the rebellion and the revelation and destruction of the man of lawlessness. We're told that Satan will be loosed for a short time. Are we in that short time right now? Is the battle what's happening now? I think the Bible is deliberately ambiguous so that Christians in every age can see things that fit the scenario and be motivated to stand fast for Christ. I think Satan is loose and he's fighting. How long will this short time last? The Bible never answers that question, but, "with the Lord a day is like a thousand years."[3] We can know for sure, however, that the war has already been won by Christ on the cross and in the resurrection.

---

[1] 2 Thess 2:3f
[2] Ancient Jews called this evil incarnate the power Belial (Deut 13:13; 1 Kgs 21:10, 13; 2 Sam 22:5)
[3] 2 Pet 3:8

Remember, neither Jesus nor John ever intended to help us identify the day and date of Jesus' return. They left that question unanswered and instead sought and still seek to encourage us with the certain knowledge of Jesus' victory.

We can prepare for the Battle of Armageddon by putting on the armor of God. God has already given us the weapons to fight this fight. We can know, believe, and love the truth. We can train in and practice righteousness, not waiting until we're under pressure or persecution to get serious. We don't prepare for the Battle of Armageddon with half-hearted attention to faith and truth. We prepare by giving it our full attention and commitment. And we can trust God.

THE GREAT TRIBULATION

Often when people talk about The Revelation you will hear mention of the Great Tribulation. "Tribulation" is a word most often translated suffering. It is so translated in 1:9; 2:9, 10, and 22. In chapter 7 one of the Elders standing around the throne of God explains to John that the worshiping multitude were those who have survived the tribulation, the great one. It's called great because it includes all the persecutions and troubles of the people of God. The Great Tribulation is a description, not a title. Rather than suggesting a specific time of persecution at a specific point in history it speaks of all the suffering of God's people at all times. The point the Elder is making is that these people have survived without giving up on Jesus.

THE SECOND COMING OF JESUS

In a prelude of His coming back Jesus said that He is going to prepare a place for us.[1] This is one of the basic doctrines of the Christian faith. Jesus is coming back to earth. Because it has been about 2000 years and He still hasn't returned, many people including Christians, doubt. Do you think some Christians you know would do some of the stuff they do if they really believed that Jesus might show up at any time? The truth is, Jesus is coming back and it may be at any time.

People who teach that Jesus can't come back until He completes

---

[1] John 14:3

certain exercises the way they understand it, have missed the whole point of The Revelation. God never intended for us to know when He is coming back. He intends for us to know that He is coming back so to be ready for Him at any time. The Revelation was written to encourage and comfort Christians however long they must wait. We're challenged to overcome doctrinal error, immorality, idolatry, complacency, rejection, and persecution. Any signs we get from The Revelation are ambiguous enough to keep all Christians living as if He might return at any moment.

In the first century many Christians were confused because they thought Jesus would return while they were still living. Some went looking for answers and some of the answers they were getting didn't come from God. As a result they developed a mistaken view of the end times, and for some, apostasy. To complicate things, they thought life should get easier for them but it actually got worse. They were being persecuted, there were doctrinal divisions in the church, and some were seduced by the culture, adopting the lifestyle of their contemporaries instead of living like Jesus.

Paul encouraged the Christians in Thessalonica to stand firm for Christ as they endured very difficult experiences, connecting God's justice with the second coming of Jesus. He said God's justice will coincide with Jesus' return.[1]

There are four things we know for sure about His return. First, it will be visible. Everyone will see Him come back. You won't miss it. No one will. John's vision began with the declaration that He's coming and every eye will see Him.[2]

Second, it will be in victory. Jesus will make all things right. This is especially important to people who are being persecuted. When Jesus came the first time He didn't come as a victor but as a suffering servant. The next time He comes it will be as the King of Kings and Lord of Lords.[3]

Third, it will be a vindication. Christians will celebrate because there'll be no more doubters. Everyone will know the truth. Many people scoff at the promise of Jesus' second coming. Peter warned about them. They'll pursue evil desires, making fun of we who believe Jesus.[4] They think we're nuts. They call us fools, and rail at us

---

[1] 2 Thess 1:7b
[2] Rev 1:7. See also Matt 24:30
[3] Rev 19:11–15
[4] 2 Pet 3:3f

and what we believe. We continue firm in faith because we know that at His second coming we'll be vindicated.[1]

Fourth, it will be sudden, like a thief coming unannounced at night.[2] The destruction of this world and its renewal will happen. When it happens, it'll happen without a new warning as if to help us quickly get ready. We have all the warning we're going to get in the Bible already. When Jesus comes back, everyone will see Him and we'll all know what's happening. Being a true follower of Jesus isn't always easy or fun but remember, Jesus said, I'll be back. Then I'll make it right.

LIFE AFTER DEATH

Several of the world's religions believe that after you die on earth you return in another form or as another person. Some believe that you're sort of absorbed into the universe. One of the primary beliefs of the Christian faith is that we continue on after we die. We either go to heaven or hell. Except for Jesus, no one has ever experienced death and returned to tell us about it.[3] Whatever we know about life after death must come from God.

Can we know with any certainty what happens to us after we die? Certainly we can. God, in the Bible, gives us five realities of what we'll experience. We'll be conscious[4] We're not just road kill. When we die we're not just gone, period. We don't just go to sleep forever. The Bible seems to indicate that after we die we're still conscious. Looking into the angelic heaven John saw the souls of people who had been martyred because of their faith. Their bodies were killed, but they were still alive, conscious in the presence of God. They remembered what they'd experienced on earth. We're not told if all Christians who die will be aware of a time span between our death on earth and entry into eternity.

We'll have no bodies. John saw their souls, but not bodies. We exist in bodies right now. Paul called our bodies, tents.[5] When we die we move out of our tents but we don't become ghosts. We have

---

[1] Titus 2:11–13
[2] 2 Pet 3:10
[3] I have not forgotten Lazarus, Jairus' daughter, and a boy returned to his mother. There is no record of them telling us about their experiences.
[4] Rev 6:9f
[5] 2 Cor 5:1

some sort of substance, enough that John was able to recognize the souls he saw.

Our souls are made perfect. This perfection doesn't mean according to human standards. The perfection of our souls has something to do with how God created us. Because of sin we're no longer perfect. We fall short of the glory of God.[1] When we become Christians God begins to heal our less than perfect souls. Christians who have died have been made perfect. They no longer sin, they no longer desire to sin.

We'll be happy. When we die on earth we go to the angelic heaven, the world of angels where God is visible to the angels, where Jesus is present seated at the right hand of God. (Remember, the final or eternal heaven does not exist yet.) The Apostle Paul recognized that when we die we'll be much happier than we can be here. He wrote that he would prefer to be away from the body and at home with the Lord.[2] Dying won't be sad for us. It'll be sad for those we leave behind (we hope), but for us it will be a happy time. This is what Jesus meant when He told the thief on the cross that he would soon be in paradise.[3] He wasn't going to purgatory.

We'll be hopeful. Hopeful because that isn't our final destination. Eternal heaven is our final destination. Until the resurrection we're not home. We're still waiting, anticipating more.

What does this have to do with the second coming of Jesus? The Bible speaks of "the Resurrection" as a particular event.[4] Why do we need the resurrection if we're already in the presence of Jesus? At the resurrection we get new bodies to be what God created us to be. It's our nature to have a body and a soul. (That's the primary difference between humans and other created beings.) To be a soul without a body isn't how God created us. When we die on earth, our souls separate from our bodies. At the resurrection we get new bodies and defeat our final enemy, the second death.

There are two groups of Christians, those who have died on earth and those who are still alive when Jesus returns. When He returns, Jesus will come bringing those who have died.[5] All those body–less souls will come with Jesus. Two things will happen. First,

---

[1] Rom 3:23
[2] 2 Cor 5:6–8; Phil 1:21–24
[3] Luke 23:43
[4] Matt 22:28; Luke 14:14
[5] 1 Thess 4:14

those souls will get new bodies. Our earthly bodies return to their natural elements. It doesn't matter what happens to our bodies because God will create new bodies. Second, those who are living will be transformed. We'll morph into new bodies[1] without the same pride issues we have now. Maybe we'll have a trunk with a head and arms and legs. Maybe we'll look like we do here on earth. There seems to be indication in the Bible that we'll at least know each other. Whatever it is, it'll be something glorious.[2]

According to 1 Corinthians 15:42–44 there are four characteristics of our new bodies. They'll be imperishable and glorious. They'll have power. Not like Superman but not subject to fatigue. And finally our new bodies will be spiritual. Right now our bodies are designed for life on earth. Our new bodies will be designed for life in eternal heaven.

THE RAPTURE

What the Bible actually says about Jesus' coming back to earth is quite different from what is often taught in churches today. Because there's so much speculation about what the Bible means the truth is often missed. Know this, and this is very important, what God inspired the writers to include in the Bible about the Second Coming of Jesus and the end of the world, was understandable to simple uneducated people who were faithful to God and needed a message of hope to sustain them through terrible persecution, cultural seduction, and false teaching.

I know of no evidence that the Christians of the churches who received The Revelation ever debated what it meant. The Christians in the seven churches of Revelation understood what John wrote. It was intended to be encouragement, not subject for speculation and argument. Because Christians were being disrespected and abused by society and governing authorities, many Christians were surrendering their faith to survive. In The Revelation God was saying, Don't quit on me. I'm coming back and when I do I will make all things right, rewarding those who love me and punishing those who disobey. The message was clear enough that Christians without special training could understand it.

A key aspect of Jesus return to earth involves what happens at

---
[1] 1 Cor 15:51f
[2] Phil 3:20f

the moment of His return, often referred to as The Rapture. Perhaps the most interesting and exciting interpretation is what Hal Lindsey wrote of what it'll be like when, as he believed, suddenly and without warning Christians will disappear as Jesus raptures them away.[1] When the rapture happens, it's not going to be like that. That is great storytelling, but it is not what the Bible says.

There's only one place in the Bible that speaks of the Rapture.[2] It's not even mentioned in The Revelation. The word rapture comes from 1 Thess 4:17, we are caught up. The Greek word is "hapazo", to snatch away. Our English word rapture comes from the Latin "rapto," to reach out and grab something, to snatch it and carry it away. Jesus said, "At that time the sign of the Son of Man will appear in the sky, and all the nations of the earth will mourn. They will see the Son of Man coming on the clouds of the sky, with power and great glory. And He will send His angels with a loud trumpet call, and they will gather His elect from the four winds, from one end of the heavens to the other."[3] Note, the angels will do the snatching. There's nothing secret about this snatching. He'll appear in the sky and everyone will see Him. As 1 Thessalonians tells us, there'll be a loud trumpet call and the voice of the archangel. When this happens it'll be loud and proud. No one's going to be looking around asking what happened.

Where did we get the crazy stuff about people suddenly disappearing and everybody left behind wondering what happened

Actually, before 1830 nobody talked about that kind of scenario. According to historian David McPherson, in Port Glasgow, Scotland, a teen–aged girl who was terribly sick with high fever went into a trance. When she recovered she told of her dream of Christians being taken away, one here, one there, etc. Somehow, this developed into the idea of a secret rapture wherein Christians

---

[1] Lindsey, p. 135f. He speculated that those who are alive will tell their story. "There I was, driving down the freeway and all of a sudden the place went crazy...cars going in all directions...and not one of them had a driver. I mean it was wild! I think we've got an invasion from outer space." "It was the last quarter of the championship game and the other side was ahead. Our boys had the ball. We made a touchdown and tied it up. The crowd went crazy. Only one minute to go and they fumbled – our quarterback recovered – he was about a yard from the goal when – zap – no more quarterback – completely gone, just like that!" "It was puzzling, very puzzling. I was teaching my course in the Philosophy of Religion when all of a sudden three of my students vanished. They simply vanished! They were quite argumentative, always trying to prove their point from the Bible. No great loss to the class. However, I do find this disappearance very difficult to explain."
[2] 1 Thess 4:13–18
[3] Matt 20:30f

disappear and those who don't know Jesus are left behind.

There are actually two raptures. One for the faithful who'll be snatched away to eternal life, and another for those who refuse God, who'll be snatched away to shame and everlasting contempt.[1] There's nothing in either Matthew, or 1 Thessalonians about sequence. In Matthew 24:36–41 Jesus did say that when He returns two men or two women will be together. One will be taken and the other left. It seems that most people assume it's the Christian who is taken, but Jesus did not say that. He mentions no sequence here. He only said one will be taken and one will be left. In fact, from Jesus' comparison with the flood of Noah we should conclude that it's the evil who are taken away like the wicked were taken away by the flood.

Consider a parable Jesus told in Matthew 13:24–30 in which a man planted his field but in the night an enemy planted weeds among his crop. When his farm hands wanted to pull up the weeds the man ordered instead to let them grow together. At the harvest the weeds will be taken up and burned first, then the crop will be gathered. Jesus explains this parable for us. "The one who sowed the good seed is the Son of Man. The field is the world, and the good seed stands for the sons of the kingdom. The weeds are the sons of the evil one, and the enemy who sows them is the devil. The harvest is the end of the age, and the harvesters are angels. As the weeds are pulled up and burned in the fire, so it will be at the end of the age. The Son of Man will send out His angels, and they will remove from His kingdom everything that causes sin and all who do evil. They will throw them into the fiery furnace, where there will be weeping and gnashing of teeth. Then the righteous will shine like the sun in the kingdom of their Father. He who has ears, let him hear."[2] In this there is sequence. There's no reason to conclude that the wicked are left behind. According to Jesus it's the other way around. The evil are taken first then the sons of the kingdom are taken.

The rapture is for the purpose of emptying the earth so that God can create a new heaven and new earth.[3] We're raptured because everything is going be burned up. God will rebuild or recreate the universe including a new heaven and new earth. Everyone will be resurrected. Some to reward and some to punishment. Those who'll

---

[1] See Dan 12:1b–f
[2] Matt 13:37–43
[3] 2 Pet 3:10, 12bf

be punished are snatched away first, then the faithful are snatched away.

JUDGMENT

We can know certain facts about the judgment to come. We know judgment will take place in the angelic heaven, where Christ sits on the throne.[1] A throne has two major purposes. The king rules from his throne, and the king judges disputes and conflicts of the people from his throne. If someone was charged with a crime, he stood before the king on his throne and the king passed judgment. We know that Jesus will be the judge. According to John, the Father has trusted the Son with authority to judge.[2] Although sometimes we're told that God judges and other times that Jesus does, the point is not to differentiate between the two. They are one and the same. It's God who judges through Christ, as opposed to being subject to the judgment of men.

We know who'll be judged. Paul wrote that sinners will be judged for stubborn and unrepentant hearts,[3] and that we'll all stand before the throne of judgement.[4] John also wrote that we also are judged. If we're faithful to Jesus we will have confidence on the Day of Judgment.[5] The believer doesn't have to worry about the outcome of the judgment but he will face the judgment. Jesus Himself said He'll sit on His throne. Everyone will gather before Him and be separated as a shepherd separates sheep and goats.[6] The separation is between those receiving reward from those who'll receive destruction. (That's one of those times early in The Revelation when the end of the world is described.[7])

We know that our conduct, every deed, every hidden thing whether good or evil, even our minds and motives will be judged.[8] In this He'll judge the validity of our faith. To make sense of this it's important that we understand the purpose of judgment. It's not to decide whether or not we're saved. God already knows that. He has known for all eternity. There are three purposes. One, judgment is to

---

[1] Rev 3:21, 4:2, 20:11; Matt 25:31
[2] John 5:22, 27
[3] Rom 2:5
[4] 1 Cor 5:10
[5] 1 John 4:17
[6] Matt 25:31f
[7] Rev 11:18
[8] Eccl 12:14; Jer 17:10; 1 Cor 4:5; 2 Cor 5:10; Rev 20:12f, 22:12

determine reward and punishment. Jesus seemed to indicate that there'll be degrees of punishment and degrees of reward.[1] I have no idea how this works. I would think if I am in heaven I am in heaven. How could it be any better? If I am in hell I am in hell. How could it be any worse? However it works, God uses the judgment to determine what we get, great reward or less reward, great punishment or less punishment.

Two, judgment is to vindicate God's justice in condemning some to hell. Of some people it's easy to think they deserve to go to hell. Their works demonstrate that they're pure evil. Others aren't so clearly deserving of eternal punishment. The judgment will vindicate God in His decision as a man is confronted with his sin and his rejection of the Savior. It will be clear of anyone directed to hell that he chose it. Very few people think they're deserving of condemnation. On judgment day we'll have nothing to say. We'll make no excuses. The Revelation is clear, it doesn't matter how important or unimportant we are. We'll all stand before the throne and the Book of Life will be opened. Everyone will be judged by what is in the books, according to what we have done. Did we believe and accept Jesus or did we deny Him? If a person's name isn't in the Book of Life, he is punished in hell.[2] Anyone who goes to hell has no argument with God. The judgment will make that clear.

Three, judgment is to glorify God in saving some even though their works would indicate that they deserve hell. God created us so that He could love us. He sent Jesus so that we could be lovable. If we are judged only according to our works, we're all indeed condemned. Not one of us is good and righteous.[3] Instead of judging us according to our deeds, He judges us according to His grace. We're saved by grace through faith.[4] In judgment there'll be no sin to judge because Jesus already paid for it. We'll know that we don't deserve it but by the amazing grace of God we'll be welcomed into heaven. In Christ there is no condemnation.[5] There is nothing scary about the judgment. We choose whether life after death will be heaven or hell. When the judgment comes it'll be clear that some people deserve to go to hell. If you have faith in Jesus your name is written in the book of life. Then you'll go into eternity with Jesus to

---

[1] Luke 12:47f, 20:47, 19:17–19
[2] Rev 20:12, 15
[3] Rom 3:10–12
[4] Eph 2:8
[5] Rom 8:1

enjoy the eternal spring of the water of life and the light of God.[1]

THE ANTI-CHRIST

The Anti–Christ is not mentioned in The Revelation. There are only four references to the Anti–Christ in the New Testament (or the entire Bible for that matter).

1 John 2:18, 22; 4:3; and 2 John 1:7

We needn't look for some individual who has special authority or impact on the events of or leading up to the second coming of Christ.

---

[1] Rev 21:6f, 21:22–27

CHAPTER FOUR
THE TEXT OF REVELATION

As you begin reading about the text of The Revelation I encourage you to have a Bible in print opened to the texts as they are discussed. This will best serve your understanding. As we read let's not lose sight of the theme of John's writing, that being to encourage his readers to remain faithful to Jesus in every circumstance whether pleasant or terrible, knowing that even though it seems that evil is winning right now, we will ultimately enjoy victory. We'll read the text in seven parts corresponding to the seven parallel sections we discussed earlier. As you read I encourage you to read it like a personal letter to you, to encourage and challenge you, as opposed to reading The Revelation as a prophecy about when the Second Coming of Christ will occur.

Part One: Chapter 1:1–3:22. John identifies Jesus who is present with His church (He walks among the lampstands) and sends letters to seven local churches. Jesus knows what they experience and will respond in appropriate measure. John is also to write what he sees in this vision and send it to the churches mentioned. Emphasis is on Jesus claiming His kingdom. The churches are encouraged and warned to hold securely to faith in Jesus Christ until the end.

Part Two: Chapter 4:1–8:5. This section describes Jesus sitting on the throne of Heaven. It begins with worship but moves on to describe terrible evil in the world. A book (scroll) with seven seals is presented that no one can open to understand history. A Lamb (also called the Lion of Judah and David's Root) appears. He is able to open the seals and the book. As the Lamb opens the seals, history from the first to the second coming of Jesus is seen. The end of the world is seen in 6:12–17 and 7:16f.

Part Three: Chapter 8:6–11:19. This section continues with the opening of the seventh seal and describes evil with ugly descriptors, including punishment for sin. There is the emergence of seven angels with seven trumpets. As each trumpet is blown God's punishment on evil is described. We are taken to the end of the world in 11:17–19.

Part Four: Chapter 12:1–14:20. Here we read about two ideologies at war. We meet the enemies of God and His servants, namely the dragon, two beasts, and the whore (government, culture, and anti–Christian religion). The dragon tried to devour the man–child of a woman clothed with the sun and the moon under her feet. The dragon is unsuccessful but there is war in Heaven between Michael with his angels (Team Jesus) fighting with Satan and his agents (Team Satan). The enemies are judged and destroyed. Again we read about the end of the world, in 14:9–20.

Part Five: 15:1–16:21. In this we read of seven bowls of the wrath God poured out on evil in the world. The world's ending is seen in 16:15–21.

Part Six: Chapters 17:1–19:21. Now the vision describes the total destruction of Satan (called Babylon) and his agents who are currently making war against the Lamb. Eventually the enemies of God, including all who follow the dragon, the beasts, and the prostitute, are judged and destroyed as clearly seen in 19:11–21.

Part Seven: Chapter 20:1–22:21. This, the last section, makes clear the final and permanent fall of Satan. Satan is bound but he does not stop fighting. When Jesus returns He brings about the ultimate defeat of Satan. There is both judgment on evil and reward for the faithful.[1] The new heaven and new earth are described with beautiful and majestic imagery. This is a final call to obedience and faithfulness because Jesus is coming with reward and punishment.[2]

PART ONE: CHAPTERS 1:1–3:22

1:1–3

We note first and foremost that this is not the revelation of when Jesus is coming back. It is the revelation of Jesus Christ. It's God's plan for the history of the world with special emphasis on the church. It's God's communication of that plan through Jesus to His

---
[1] Rev 21:7f
[2] Rev 22:7, 12,20

angel through John to us.

John introduces himself and the occasion of this vision, and offers a blessing about this message. God blesses whoever reads the words of prophecy. This probably refers to the one who reads in public session. Most people could not read at that time so they were dependent on a reader. I would suggest that there is blessing for whoever reads this message whether to a group (congregation) or for him or herself.

The message is called words of prophecy. Remember, prophecy isn't about predicting. It means to tell forth. Sometimes prophecy includes a predictive element, but the purpose of prophecy is to declare God's Word. Blessed also is whoever hears and heeds[1] the message, who continually hears the Word and who continually obeys. Specifically they read and heed what is written. The Greek verb form means it's done. The Word of God in The Revelation is finished and there will be no more. It is vitally important that we hear and obey because the time is near. Time is the word "καιρος." Had he used "χρονος" (chronology) it would suggest a time line. Καιρος refers to an era, a fixed period. The era of The Revelation is now.

1:4–8

Verses 4–7 seem to be John's editorial, not necessarily part of the vision. The writer is John the Apostle, the guy who wrote the Gospel and three short letters. John will send this revelation to the seven churches mentioned but it was certainly intended for all of Jesus' followers in all times to read and obey. John uses a common salutation grace and peace to you. This grace and peace are from Jesus who was and is and is to come. That three–fold designation of Christ is used throughout this letter. Also mentioned are the seven spirits before the throne, referring to the Holy Spirit in His fullness (7 indicates completeness). Jesus is further referred to as the faithful witness, the medium of the Revelation. He has delivered it without any modification to appease the mind of man. In his gospel, John emphasized Jesus' role as witness. Jesus told Nicodemus He speaks of truth of what He has seen.[2] Jesus told Pilate that He was born for this purpose, to testify to the truth.[3] As a witness Jesus spoke from

---
[1] The Greek word is variously translated keep, observe, obey, pay attention. Clearly it means to put the message into daily practice.

[2] John 3:11

[3] John 18:37

first–hand knowledge. Having come from God He is uniquely able to tell us about God. Faithful witness is Jesus' ministry on earth.

He's also the firstborn of the dead, a descriptive word picture of a vital aspect of His Messianic work, expressing His absolute and final victory over death. Others have been raised from the dead but only Jesus' body would never die again. Through His resurrection from the dead it was declared that He is the Son of God.[1] Being firstborn creates two thoughts. One, He is the first to defeat death. And two, like a first born son who inherited his father's honor and power Jesus has all the power, authority, and honor of God.

He is called the ruler of the kings of the earth, what Jewish scholars have always understood to be a description of the Messiah.[2] Used here it's a claim that Jesus is the Messiah. When Jesus was tempted by the Devil, the Devil offered Him authority over all the kingdom of the world.[3] What the devil promised he couldn't deliver but Jesus earned by dying on the cross and rising from the dead

He's called who was, who is, who is to come, as when God told Moses His name.[4] Who was, continues to be. This expression is essentially a proper name for Jesus, expressing His unchangeable nature. He is Almighty God.

Something of a short doxology interrupts these word pictures of Jesus to speak of what He did for us. He set us free from our sin by His blood. We've been in bondage to sin, sin controlled us, but we've been set free at the price of His blood. He is constantly loving us. His love is already active and endures forever. He made us a kingdom and priests, reminiscent of Exodus 19:6 where God said Israel would be a kingdom of priests.[5] Most religions believe that only certain individuals have access to their god. Because of what Jesus did, access to God is not limited to a chosen few. It's an open invitation to every person. Martin Luther called this the priesthood of all believers.

John adds this declaration about Jesus. He is coming again and every eye will see Him. No one will miss this event. Jesus is coming back and when He does it's not going to be a secret. Every eye will physically see Jesus, including all those who pierced Him. "Those

---

[1] Rom 1:4
[2] Psalm 89:27
[3] Luke 4:5–7
[4] Ex 3:14
[5] What used to be used of Israel (Ex 19:6) is now used of those who believe Jesus.

who" represents people of all ages and all times who reject Jesus.[1] Zechariah wrote that people will mourn the one they have pierced.[2] The verb for mourn suggests visual grief. You get the image of a crowd of men beating on their chests because they have rejected the only one who can forgive their sins. What incites this mourning is judgment. When Jesus comes back, playtime is over.

John ends this depiction of Jesus with a rather Walter Cronkite like expression, "So shall it be, Amen." He then interjects the words of Jesus Himself.[3] "I am the Alpha and the Omega, who is, and who was, and who is to come, the Almighty."

1:9–11

John calls himself a brother (a common reference of Christians one to another), and a companion or partaker in tribulation.[4] Remember this the next time someone tells you that there is a particular period of suffering called the tribulation that is yet to come. John thought he and they were already experiencing the tribulation. John also presents himself as part of the Kingdom just like they were. Finally, just like they were doing, he was patiently enduring, holding on to faith against intense persecution. John had been exiled to Patmos, a prison island about 100 miles southwest of Ephesus, used by the Romans for people they wanted out of the picture but were not interested in killing.

He was worshiping when Jesus spoke to him.[5] His worship led John to shift from contact with the physical world to a state of what he called being in the spirit. What he now sees he sees not with physical eyes. It is now that he received his commission. His attention had been won by the sound of a trumpet.[6] He was told to write the visions he was about to experience. He was to send his writing to seven particular churches. The visions demonstrate Jesus' role in history and in the great struggle between God and evil.

---

[1] Isa 53:5
[2] Zech 12:10
[3] A Red Letter addition of the Bible rightly puts these word in red.
[4] See the discussion about tribulation in chapter three.
[5] It was the Lord's Day, the day we commemorate Jesus' resurrection.
[6] A trumpet was commonly used to get the attention of whomever God wanted to hear His message (Ex 19:16, 19; Lev 25:9; Josh 6:5; Isa 58:1).

1:12–16

John saw Jesus clothed in power and majesty and awe and terror. We need to see Jesus like John saw Jesus. He speaks with a voice like a trumpet that thunders across the land. His words bring comfort to those who love Him and terror to those who do evil (see 2:16). His power is unsurpassed. His appearance is like the sun. We cannot be casual in the presence of such a one. We must, like John, fall before Him as though dead.[1] Jesus is a coming judge who will cause intense wailing, except for those who have accepted Him as Savior and surrendered to Him as Lord.

Compare this to what many Christians today think of Jesus. To some He's simply the Lamb of God. If He is the Lion of Judah He's been declawed. There is little sense of awe, or reverence, or fear, even among many in the church today. That's not what we see in The Revelation. If you don't see Jesus in His fullness I encourage you to spend some time in The Revelation. Let God's own Word show you who Jesus is. When you see Him clearly, you'll never be flippant or casual. You won't be lukewarm. If you're not excited about Jesus, you're not seeing Him clearly. When you see Him like John saw Him, you won't need anyone to motivate you. You'll follow Him out of love for what He has done for you and out of a desire to be among those who gather around His throne to worship rather than one of those who beat their breasts in defeat.

The one John saw, who he referred to as a Son of Man was walking among seven golden lampstands. These are the seven churches identified in verse 11. As lampstands they symbolize the church's role in being light bearers to the world.[2]

1:17–20

What John saw overwhelmed him. Jesus lifted him up and told him not to be afraid but to write what he sees and hears, again referring to Himself as who was and is and is to come. He holds the keys to death and Hades.[3]

Seven churches are identified as immediate recipients of what John writes. Jesus knew these churches well. He knew that they were

---

[1] Rev 1:17
[2] Matt 5:14
[3] Hendriksen says of Hades that it "signifies a state of disembodied existence...that results when life ceases and when body and soul separate." P. 67

struggling with the forces trying to force them from faithfulness to Christ. The letters address specific issues they faced. These churches were marked by apathy, immorality, sloppy teaching, and complacency, but none–the–less, Jesus loved them. Even though they were messy, just like many churches today, He loved them as He loves today's troubled churches. It's tough love, but it is real love. He challenges, corrects, and confronts local congregations and individual Christians, aiming to bring them to greater maturity. The Bible says God disciplines those He loves.[1] He certainly loves the church because He disciplines her. I believe that if we listen carefully to these nuggets of discipline they'll encourage growth among us in our churches.

Notice as we read the letters we see that these congregations aren't perfect but they're His and He loves them. Jesus wanted these Christians to desire something more than what the world offers. He wanted them to yearn for Heaven that truly satisfies. This calls for a new way to look at life, seeing more of the eternal and less of the here and now. He will encourage them to overcome persecution, cultural seduction, and false teaching.

If we see Jesus for who He is, the suffering servant with power and authority who is the promised Savior, we will worship Him in all circumstances, even suffering. We'll witness of Him and, recognizing evil, seek to keep ourselves pure.

The letters are not in parentheses. They're important and form the foundation for the rest of The Revelation. Some interpreters have suggested that the letters are not to specific churches but to certain periods of church history. I disagree! They were specific churches in specific cities.

The letters are directed to the angel of each church. The word angel refers, as it does some 60 times in the Revelation, to a created being employed in the service of God (although I am kind of partial to the idea that angel refers to the preacher of the church). "When John uses the word Αγγελος he does not use it in the sense of messenger; he uses it in the sense of angel."[2] Hendriksen maintains that the angels of the churches are in fact the ministers/pastors of the individual churches.[3] I am unable to support Hendriksen's view. If Αγγελος means the guardian angel of each congregation that

---
[1] Heb 12:6
[2] Barclay, 67
[3] Henricksen, p 68, 73

would present a problem. If it is to the guardian angel of the church then it is the guardian angel who is being warned and challenged for the sins of the churches. I am not confident in either of those interpretations. However I can't offer a better suggestion.

There's so much good stuff in these letters that we mustn't give them a superficial glance, so we'll look closely at each one. The letters follow a pattern although they are not exactly the same. Each includes a salutation, who the letter is written to, Jesus' self-designation, commendation, condemnation, warning and threat, and exhortation. And there is promise.

As we examine the letters look for the examples of persecution, cultural seduction, and false teaching.

2:1–7

The church in Ephesus was one of the Apostle Paul's favorites. He stopped there for a time on one of his missionary journeys.[1] It's not known how old this church was but, since Acts 18 is the first mention of Christian activity in Ephesus, I would suggest this is when the church was founded. When Paul moved on he left Priscilla and Aquila, a capable husband and wife team, to lead the church. Later he returned to Ephesus finding many disciples. After Paul got into debates about Jesus in the Jewish synagogue he moved his discussions to the lecture hall of Tyrannus for two years. People throughout the province heard about Jesus.[2] His mission was so successful making new disciples of Jesus that some merchants who earned money selling idol related merchandise got other merchants riled up starting a riot. A little while after this riot, when Paul's mission work was winding down, he called for the Elders of the church in Ephesus to say farewell and offer one last word of encouragement. (This is one of the passages from which we learn about Elders in the NT.[3])

Ephesus was a wealthy and prosperous city. Sort of the New York City of Asia. The harbor could handle the largest of ships. Several highways converged in Ephesus. The church in Ephesus was probably around 40 years old when this letter was written.

Jesus identified Himself as the one holding the seven stars and

---

[1] Acts 18:18–21
[2] Acts 19:10
[3] Acts 20:17ff

walking among the seven golden lampstands. The stars have already been identified as the angels[1] and the lampstands are the churches themselves. Jesus walks among them. That's His way of saying: I'm there. I know what's going on. He's clear that He knows their hard work and their perseverance. This is an active congregation. They work hard doing what churches do.[2] Being a church is never for the lazy. It's hard work and Jesus praised the church in Ephesus for it.

He praised their perseverance. One of the keys to understanding The Revelation is to keep in mind that these people were being persecuted for being Christians. The persecution was not that they lacked A/C, or that the parking lot was crowded, or that church time was inconvenient. They were thrown to wild dogs and lions in the arena for sport. They were burned at the stake, crucified, and boiled in giant cauldrons, but most would not give up on being the church.

Jesus praised their intolerance, that they did not tolerate evil people. In those days there were people who taught Christians to obey the Jewish law rather than the Gospel. There were libertines, who taught freedom and license. Your behavior didn't matter because you're free in Christ. Do whatever you want. Christ forgives. There were beggars who preyed on the charity of churches. Jesus praised the church for testing people who tried to claim the authority of God when they taught false doctrine.[3] The church in Ephesus was morally alert. Paul warned of all this when he said Good-bye to the Elders.[4]

One more praise did the Lord offer. He praised them that they've not grown weary under pressure. Think about the courage it would take when some of your church members are arrested and tortured. How long would any of us last? Jesus said, You didn't grow weary. Persecution didn't wear them out. Because they worked hard they were not dissuaded by the pressure.

That is an amazing church. What could possibly be wrong with a congregation like that? Well, Jesus found that they lost their first love. Forsake is a powerful word meaning to let go, give away, cancel, or abandon. It's in active voice which means it's something someone does, not something that happens to someone. This wonderful,

---

[1] Rev 1:20
[2] Paul used the same word for work in Romans 16:12 referencing Tryphena and Tryphosa who work hard in the Lord. Of himself Paul claimed in 1 Cor 15:10, by God's grace, to work harder than others.
[3] 1 Thess 5:19–22; 1 Cor 14:29
[4] Acts 20:29–31

hardworking, persecution enduring, congregation who continually toiled at the stuff churches do, it seems, weren't devoted to Christ as much as to being a church. They were like a husband and wife whose love has decayed but out of a sense of duty they remain faithful. If that sense of duty fails, they divorce. Sometimes Christian people, for whatever reason, stop loving Jesus the way they used to. They're just not as devoted as they used to be so they divorce Jesus. Jesus said to them, I hold this against you.

Part of the value of studying these letters is that the issues those Christians experienced are, except for the severe persecution, the same issues we tend to experience. It's not unusual to find churches and Christians who are committed to being a church but not with the love they used to have. They don't often drop out completely nor do they drop out all of a sudden. It's usually a slow process but in the end they are much different than they were before. They don't worship as often. They cease doing acts of service. They stop using the gifts God gave them for the common good. Basically, they forsake being true followers of Jesus and turn into fans at best and apathetic acquaintances at worst.

In His letter Jesus told them how to repair their relationship. This is good for Christians today who have lost that sense of excitement and gratefulness for salvation in Christ. First, they should remember what they were before. Memory is a good first step back when you have fallen away. The Prodigal Son in Jesus' parable forsook his father's house and values and ran off to sow his wild oats. As Jesus tells the story, when he "remembered" that his father's servants were better off than he was he decided to go home. If you're not close to God it wasn't God who moved. If you're not feeling it, it's not the church's fault. Remember where you came from.

Second, Repent. You know what it means. Turn around. Stop not loving Jesus. Turn back to your love. Whatever it takes, get back to where you really love Jesus and you're not just going through the motions.

Third, return to what they were. The sorrow of repentance isn't supposed to drive us to despair. It's meant to cause us to surrender to the grace of God and then to get back to doing what we did before.

Something you should know about these three steps, each one is singular. It's not a group thing even though the whole group may be guilty. It's an individual response. Each person, accept responsibility for falling away. Remember where you came from. Repent and go back to where you were before. They needed to follow this prescription in the church in Ephesus. This is serious to Jesus if not to us. In His tough love He issued this threat, Repent or perish. Apparently they didn't take Him seriously because there is no Christian church in Ephesus today.

After the warning and threat we get another commendation. Jesus saw that they hated the sins of the Nicolaitans. In Acts 6 we read about a problem that came up in the church in Jerusalem in that certain widows weren't being treated equally by those who were in charge of distributing food to the needy. The Apostles urged the people to select seven men who were filled with the Spirit and wisdom to take the responsibility of being deacons in charge of food distribution. One of the men the church chose was Nicolas from Antioch. It seems he forsook his first love.

Hippolytus, an ancient historian wrote, "He departed from correct doctrine and was in the habit of teaching indifference of food and life." In other words, Do whatever you want, it doesn't matter. Perhaps eat, drink, and be merry. Irenaeus wrote of the Nicolaitans. They lived lives of unrestrained indulgence. Clement also repeated the charge. They abandoned themselves to pleasure like goats. Goats don't think about what they do as if there was a moral standard by which they would be judged. Goats just do what pleases themselves. This teaching wasn't from outside. It came from inside the church. The Nicolaitans believed that the body meant nothing so you could pursue whatever pleasures you want with no spiritual implications. Not only did they participate in the same sins as the unbelievers, they justified themselves that it was OK for Christians. Do whatever brings you pleasure, as long as you believe in Jesus, you're OK.

Jesus said, I hate that. It really bothers Jesus when people, especially those who claim to be Christians, do whatever pleases them, disregarding His teaching. He hates it. That's pretty strong language, but it is what He said. Jesus does not look kindly on Christians who ignore His morality.

Finally Jesus ended His letter with this warning and promise, He who has an ear, let him hear what the Spirit says to the churches. To who overcomes, I will give the right to eat from the tree of life, which is in the paradise of God. There's a sense of urgency in His words. Each individual is addressed. Whoever has an ear listen up! Too often Christians listen only to the stuff they like and ignore the rest. Jesus suggests that we're responsible to listen to everything He teaches. And this is about active listening. You're equally responsible to prepare yourself to hear God's Word as the preacher/teacher is to prepare to deliver it. If you come to worship with your mind scattered you need to get focused. That's why most churches sing for a while before they get into the Word. They're using the songs, both the words and the music, to purge their minds of the clutter so they can tune into and hear God's Word.

The promise is offered to those who overcome, those who fight against evil and win. The final reward is the right to eat of the tree of life. This is a recurrent theme in the Revelation.[1] You'll get all the promises of the Bible if you give yourself to Jesus and stay faithful to Him until the end.

2:8–11

Throughout Christian history there has been persecution against followers of Jesus. The fact that in America we are not hotly persecuted is an aberration. Severe persecution is the background of Jesus' letter to the church in the city of Smyrna. Smyrna was known for being loyal to the Emperor and faithful in Emperor worship. It was a "Free City" of the Roman Empire meaning they had fewer restrictions than other cities.

When Jesus identified Himself as one who died and came to life again it created a positive image in the minds of Symrnites whose city had been destroyed in 600 BC and rebuilt in 200 BC. Smyrna boasted of its Golden Street lined with temples to Aphrodite, Asklepios, Apollo, and Zeus. The Christian church in Smyrna was probably founded by Paul about 53-56 AD on his third mission trip.[2] There's a particularly interesting story about persecution in Smyrna. A disciple of the Apostle John, Polycarp, was the minister of the church in Smyrna until he was burned at the stake in 155 AD. The city was filled with visitors who had come for the public games, a

---

[1] Rev 22:2, 14, 19
[2] Acts 19:10

time when many Christians were killed as sport for the masses to enjoy. Polycarp had managed to escape capture until a slave, under torture, revealed his hiding place. When they came to arrest him, Polycarp ordered those with him to provide a meal for the soldiers.

At his trial he was offered freedom if he would declare that Caesar is Lord. In response he said, For eighty six years have I served Him, and He never did me any injury. How can I now blaspheme my King and my Savior? As they continued to pressure him he said, Since you are vainly urgent that I should swear by the fortunes of Caesar, and pretend not to know who and what I am, hear me declare with boldness, I am a Christian! The Roman proconsul threatened, I have wild beasts I will throw you to unless you repent. I will burn you with fire. Polycarp said, You threaten me with fire that burns for an hour, and afterward is extinguished, but you are ignorant of the fire of the coming judgment and of eternal punishment reserved for the ungodly. Why do you tarry? The fire was then ignited.

That's the context in which Jesus gave this letter to John. Jesus identified Himself as the first and the last, one who was dead but is now alive (Vs. 8). This captures expressions used earlier about Jesus being the Alpha and Omega, the one who is, and who was, and who is coming. He says, I know what you face. He knows their persecution. Christians in Smyrna weren't waiting for the tribulation. It was already in full force. They were being arrested and forced to worship Caesar or suffer being burned to death or thrown to savage animals to be mauled, their flesh shredded and eaten.

Jesus knows their extreme poverty. There was real sacrifice in being Christian. They had nothing. They lost their jobs and were unable to sell in the market place. It's tough to remain positive when there are no physical signs of blessing. Jesus reminded them, You are rich. Not in material possessions that you can't take with you, but in spiritual possessions, grace, love, joy, and peace. All things you can take into eternity.

Jesus knows how they are being slandered by the Jews. Many Jews had taken residence in Smyrna due in part to the business environment. They didn't like the teaching that Jesus was God, so they stirred up hatred against Christians. There are several incidents in Acts where the Jews got people worked up because the Christians were saying that Jesus is the Messiah. In Paul's letters he mentions people from the circumcision party who followed his mission trips telling the new Christians that they had to become Jews before they could be saved. Maybe worst of all, they made false accusations to the Romans so that the Romans would in turn punish Christians. They accused Christians of cannibalism (communion), immorality (love feasts/fellowship dinners), breaking up families, atheism (not bowing to Caesar), disloyalty to Rome, and inciting panic (teaching about the end times). The Romans didn't need much incentive to come down hard on Christians. What kind of faith would it take to stand firm in the face of such treatment? How long would any of us last if, as a direct result of accepting Christ, the people in our lives disowned us, our employers fired us, our friends and relatives said things to hurt us, and the government tortured us? Jesus called the Jews a synagogue of Satan, saying that when Jews got together for church they were dedicated not to God but to Satan. Certainly that does not sound like the people of God.

Don't worry even though some will be tested in prison. The persecution they faced was not as simple as disgruntled Jews and sadistic Romans. Behind the persecution was the Devil himself, called Diabolos. The word translates into English, the accuser. In Jewish law, when a man was accused of a crime, the accuser stood at his right hand, declaring his crime. Satan is the one who accuses of sin.

This really is not a very comforting message. The tribulation they faced was no accident. Satan initiated persecution with a purpose, to tempt Christians to fall away. The word translated tempt means to test someone or something to determine purity, like you would test gold or silver. Jesus was saying to the church in Smyrna, The suffering you're experiencing is a test instigated by Satan. As with Job, the plan was to tempt them to turn from faith in Jesus. I don't see Satan hiding behind every tree, but I believe he has a hand in some of the things that inflict us, the things we might call tribulation. His aim is not to prove the purity of our faith but to cause us to turn from faith. It does separate serious believers from people who are not. Satan knows it doesn't work to attack the Gospel or the church, but if he can put enough personal pressure on individuals, sometimes they grow weary and give up.

When you struggle, instead of thinking that maybe Christian faith is foolishness, think about how Satan might be testing you. Are you really hooked on Jesus? Do you truly love Him more than the things of this world? Is your faith in Christ secure against even yourself? Satan wants you to give up and ask, What difference does it make? He wants you to say Caesar is Lord, or money is Lord, or health is Lord, or anything else but Jesus is Lord.

Jesus said, Don't fear. They were suffering tribulation with more to come and He said, Don't fear? Yes, He did. In fact, He added that it was the devil who would test them. Imprisonment for the Christians of Smyrna was more than going to jail. It was a prelude to death. If they got arrested, they would not be coming out except to be executed.

The persecution is not unlimited. "Ten days" was an expression for a short time which would soon come to an end. More persecution is coming but it will be short. When you're going through tribulation, no time seems short. Days drag on and on and your suffering seems never to end. The point is, compared to eternity, anything we face in this life is of a short time. The message to the Christians in Smyrna and for us is, Don't let tribulation get the best of you. Satan is trying to get you to quit on Jesus. Don't give up. Be faithful even to the point of death. Be faithful is singular. He's talking to individual Christians. You be faithful to the end. There's no promise of life for anyone who quits, even if you quit because of terrible tribulation. This is a consistent theme throughout the New Testament.[1]

Two rewards are mentioned for those who don't give up. First is the crown of life. There are two words for crown in the New Testament. A diadem is a royal crown or tiara like the one Miss America wears. The word used here is a wreath, like that given to a winner of the Olympic Games. It is a crown of victory and joy. Christians who remain faithful to the end will receive a crown of victory and joy.

The second reward is that you won't be hurt by the second death. This is an unusual phrase. In the New Testament it is found only in the Revelation.[2] To say that whoever overcomes the tribulation won't be harmed by the second death is precisely what Paul said in Romans that we who are faithful are more than victors. Nothing in this life, nothing in time or eternity, can separate us from

---

[1] Matt 10:22; 24:9–13; Luke 21:19
[2] Rev 20:6, 14; 21:8

Jesus' love.[1] A faithful man is safe from all that life can do to him and safe from all that death can do to him. By implication, the one who does not overcome, the one who gives up, will be hurt by the second death.

When you're going through something hard and wonder, "Where is God?" remember, the teacher is always quiet during a test. There's a lot of wisdom in that. The tests we face aren't beyond God's influence and control. Just because He doesn't act when and the way we want Him to doesn't mean He's not there or that He's impotent. Don't be afraid of what you experience. Be faithful and you'll receive a victor's crown of life. Tribulation you experience is difficult but it's not wasted. God will use it to separate the real followers of Jesus from the pretenders. If you overcome the tribulation, even if it hurts now, you'll not be hurt by the second death. You'll receive the victor's crown of life.

2:12–17

God has a way of putting the faith decision in simple terms we can understand. Choose me, or choose something else; no compromise; no waffling; no flip–flopping![2] Why do you suppose God issued that challenge to His people over and over again? Why not say it once and leave it? It was because even though God chose them to be His people, and did everything necessary to make them so, they had a habit of trying to choose God and the gods of other nations like Baal, Ashteroth, and Molech. They wanted the blessings that come with being God's people but at the same time the comfort of being like everybody else. They didn't want to stand out or be different. They liked the culture. They liked the ways of the culture, the things other people did and the way they did them. So they compromised. Although they prayed to Jehoveh and worshipped at His synagogue or Temple, they found that life was a lot easier when they joined in. That's the context of this letter to the church in Pergamum.

Pergamum, which boasted of a library of over 200,000 volumes, was the Capitol city of Roman Asia. They saw themselves as the defenders of the Greek way of life. It was a center of Emperor worship, with temples dedicated to Caesar, Zeus, and Asclepios (god

---
[1] Rom 8:35–39
[2] Deut 30:19; Josh 24:14f; 1 Kgs 18:21

of healing). That prompted Jesus to say it's a city where Satan lives. It's much easier to be Christian in an environment among like-minded people, but the duty of the Christian is to be a witness for Christ wherever life has set him. The Christians in the church at Pergamum had to be Christians where Satan was ensconced.

The choice for them was clear. Team Jesus or Team Satan? There was no neutral position. Their culture urged them to burn incense and say Caesar is Lord but they refused. They were truly Christians. Jesus said, I know how you suffer for it. He was aware of the tribulation they faced. He was aware that they held fast to His name. That verb means to grasp and hold on tightly. They chose to be called Christians, a name intended as a slur but they happily chose the name, and as Jesus said here, they held on tightly to it. Anyone who knew them knew they were Christians. Even persecution couldn't change their minds, not even when Antipas was murdered. We know next to nothing about this man, however Tertullian reported that when he refused to deny that Jesus is Lord, he was put in a bronze bull and roasted over a fire. Clearly these are outspoken, brave, positively stubborn Christian people.

Jesus called Himself Him who has the sharp double-edged sword. In Roman law, certain governors were granted ius gladii, The right of the sword. That gave them the legal power to have someone killed on the spot. The proconsul in Pergamum had ius gladii and at any moment might use it against the Christians. The Romans might be satanically powerful, but Jesus is more powerful still. Jesus turned that double-edged sword on them.

Never-the-less! Jesus said He had some problems with this brave church that wore His name. They had people among them who were trying to live in cognitive dissonance. They believed that Jesus is Lord but lived like someone or something else was lord. They tried to have it both ways. They held tightly to the name Jesus but held just as tightly to the teaching of Balaam for example. In Hebrew history and tradition Balaam stood for someone who is sexually immoral and follows the ways of other gods. Instead of obeying God's standards they followed the Greek way of living even though it went against God's Word.

Some held tightly to the teachings of the Nicolaitans. We discussed this in the letter to the church in Ephesus. The Nicolaitans believed that the body meant nothing so you could do whatever you want with no spiritual implications. If it was easier for business purposes to ignore the things of God or to engage in some strange religious behaviors, that was acceptable. You certainly wouldn't want to lose your job because you were a Christian. You wouldn't want to be outcast because of your personal faith. Nothing you did in the flesh mattered. Even if your morality followed the standards of a different god, since that god isn't really God, no sweat.

That was a dangerous compromise. They were trying to be Christians and at the same time live like the world. Does this sound at all familiar? Jesus was speaking to anyone trying to have it both ways. You can't do that. You can't say you believe in Me and at the same time live like those who don't believe in Me! That would be cognitive dissonance. He is calling for a faith decision. Choose Jesus or choose the world, but you cannot choose both, and He hates it when people try. Remember what Jesus said in the letter to the church in Ephesus, that He hates the teaching of the Nicolaitans. He hates it when people who claim to be Christians disregard His teaching and do whatever pleases them. Strong language? Yes, but that's what He said. Jesus hates when Christians ignore His morality.

So He called for people to repent. As He did so often in these letters, He again spoke in the singular. You repent! If you believe in Jesus, having accepted Him as Savior, but are living like the world, you need to repent! If you don't when He comes back He'll fight with you with that double–edged sword. The Bible is clear that the sword of Christ is His Word. When He comes back He'll fight with people who ignored His teaching, using His Word, the very Bible we hold, as a sword. Jesus intends to fight with Christians who ignore His teaching in some areas while holding fast to His name.

As with previous letters He finished with a personal call to individuals, not to groups. Listen to what the Spirit says. Whoever is victorious, who overcomes the troubles you face being Christian in a pagan world, are promised hidden manna and a white stone. The hidden manna reference probably comes from a legend from about 596 BC when the Temple of Solomon was destroyed. It is said Jeremiah took the pot of manna that was kept in the Temple and hid it in a cave on Mt. Sinai. When the Messiah came the manna would be discovered. So the legend goes, to eat of the hidden manna meant that a person would enjoy all the blessings of the Messianic age.

No one can say what the white stone means for sure. There are at least five or six different interpretations, all which sound good, but none can claim authority, other than to say that it is somehow a mark of identification given to faithful Christians. The new name is probably related to being permanently identified with Jesus.[1]

2:18–29

No one is drafted into the Kingdom of God. If you're a Christian, it's because you chose to be a follower of Jesus having accepted Him as your Lord and Savior. If you make that choice, you need to know what Jesus expects. None of the Christians in The Revelation were drafted into the Kingdom of God. He expected that they would put their hearts into their faith. He expected them to know and follow His will and His commands. So when they did things contrary to His will and commands, He called them out.

Significant for understanding the issue Jesus will bring against the city of Thyatira is the presence of trade guilds. There were associations for wool makers, linen makers, garment makers, those who dyed cloth, leather makers, and potters.[2] If you wanted to get ahead in life, you joined one of the guilds. That's where you made your business contacts, advertised your merchandise, and made your friends.

Every guild had their own god and membership implied worship of that god. As a faithful guild member you attended the meetings, participated in the feasts in honor of that god including eating the meals with the other members, and engaged in sexual practices that Jesus called immoral. When you became a Christian you had to choose. You could quit the guild and be an outcast which made it very difficult to do business, or you could compromise the teaching of Jesus. That was a tough choice for a Christian.

This wasn't about someone telling them they couldn't be Christians. It was about seducing them to compromise in order to get along. They could remain Christians but they also must participate in worship of the gods of the guilds. It's not unlike what we see today. Many people think, you can be a Christian without being a fanatic. Just go along to get along. Don't be intolerant of others. It's no big deal, and besides, a lot of other Christians are

---

[1] Rev 7:3; 14:1; 20:4; 22:4
[2] Lydia, the first convert to Christianity from Asia was a cloth dyer from Thyatira.

doing it.

Jesus said of this congregation. I know what you're all about: your good works, your unselfish love, your ministry, your faith, your endurance, your perseverance, and I know that your ministry is growing, you're doing more than before. That's high praise for a church. If you go to a church–related seminar today you'll meet a speaker who leads a church like that. The introductory pamphlet will talk about the work and ministry of the church, his church. It will mention how they faithfully worked through difficult circumstances and it'll tell you how much they are growing.

Jesus commended the church in Thyatira for not living in the past. They were forward thinking, not satisfied with what they used to do. They were creating new forms of ministry, new ways to express Jesus' love, new ways to reach their world with the Gospel. Couldn't Jesus just let them enjoy the praise? No, He couldn't. They weren't draftees. They were volunteers. They chose Jesus and He expected better of them. He expected them to honor Him by turning away from the sinful practices of their culture, not join in. Probably not everybody in that church but at least some of them compromised faith in order to get along. It's interesting that He didn't go after the sin itself. Rather He called the church out for permitting it. You tolerate this heresy. You tolerate is singular and present tense, meaning you continually tolerate Jezebel.

This imagery takes us back to 1 Kings. Jezebel was the wife of King Ahab of Israel, an evil witch of a woman intent on satisfying her own pleasures at everyone else's expense. Instead of helping her husband lead God's people to honor God she encouraged him to lead them into all kinds of sin. Jesus calls her a deceiver who is continually teaching and misleading Jesus' servants into sexual immorality and idol worship.

Jesus didn't intend to indicate an actual person who was leading the people in Thyatira astray, although there undoubtedly was one or more. He was talking about a mindset represented by Jezebel. It seems an acceptable solution to the problem of how to get along with the trade guilds while being Christian was to join in, participate in the sinful behaviors of the trade guilds and still be Christian. You could join in the worship of a particular trade god, or you could commit sexually immorality, and Jesus wouldn't mind.

Jesus said He intends to act against whoever teaches this

garbage. He has given Jezebel an opportunity to repent but she refuses. He said He would throw her and all who follow her onto a bed of suffering. Not just any suffering. This is mega–tribulation. Many Christians were already being persecuted, but that's nothing compared to what they'll get in hell. Judgment awaits Christians who compromise and will not repent. Repentance isn't penance. It's not merely being sorry for some sin. A good translation is, Unless they repent out of her ways. True repentance results in changed behavior. In this case, changing out of Jezebel's ways into God's ways. Unless Christians who follow this philosophy change their behavior, I will kill them in death. The double image of killing in death may refer to both the first and the second death that awaits all evil.

His actions will convince churches that He means business, that we'll reap what we sow. Some translations read that He searches the reins and hearts. Reins is a specific word that translates, kidneys. In Hebrew writing the organs were used to refer to the seat of thoughts and feelings. The point is that Jesus looks deep into our hidden motives. If we rationalize our sin, He knows. Nothing gets by Him. Each person will get what he has coming.

To those in Thyatira who had not compromised their faith, who hadn't personally experienced the deep things of Satan, that is, the cult philosophies that dominated so much of the world at that time, He offers no more burden. They don't have to defeat Satan. They just have to resist him.

Verse 25 offers this encouragement, Never–the–less I have a bit of advice. Hold on to your faith. Don't give up. Notice He didn't say that He would take away their suffering or inconvenience. Living for Jesus in the midst of a culture that spurns Him will always be difficult. For the faithful believer, this is the only hell they'll ever experience. For the unfaithful, this is only the beginning.

I have counseled many people who were facing difficult circumstances. This is where I get my wisdom. Sometimes the best you can do is hang in there. How long should Christians hang in there? Until I come! Jesus said. What it means is, and this is important, especially for those who think the Revelation is intended to tell us when Jesus is coming back, the time for Jesus to come back has even now not yet been determined. Jesus said, I'm coming back sometime, so hang in there until I do.

He made promises to those who hang in there and remain faithful. The guy who used to be a good church member but doesn't hold on isn't afforded these promises.[1] The one who is continually overcoming and continually keeping His words until God's will is complete, will receive these promises. Whoever holds firmly to the things of Christ will get what He promised. Whoever compromises Christian living for the convenience of fitting in with our culture will get the same fate as Jezebel.

Two promises are given here. One, we'll receive power over the nations. The tables will be turned. Right now the world oppresses the Christian. Faithful Christians will be associated with Christ who judges the world and condemns the sinner. And two, He'll give us the morning star. That is, we'll share in the glory and splendor of Christ.

Jesus expects faithfulness. One of the greatest threats we face is that we might compromise Christian living in order to get along with our culture. We all have principles we live by. Some are non–negotiable, that is, we'll never compromise them for any reason. Any time we compromise what we know Jesus expects of us we are in danger of falling away from Him. The first step is the most dangerous. When you take that first step away from what Jesus expects, it will lead you to more sin and ultimately to destruction. Your enemy lies. He says, A little bit isn't going to hurt you. You can handle this one little thing. But even a little bit will hurt you. Compromise usually begins as one step, one insignificant movement. It's easy to underestimate the danger. Compromise usually is not a giant act of disobedience. It's usually a minor change, a little thing that doesn't have immediate negative consequences. It's easy to rationalize that it's acceptable for a Christian to do this.

Every little accommodation weakens your conscience and makes it even easier to take another step. Each step after that becomes easier still. Also, compromise in one area of life makes it easier to compromise in other areas. Soon you're neck deep in sin and you can't seem to stop. Compromise not only leaves you vulnerable to Satan, it weakens your character. Do not think that the people in your life don't notice that you gave in a little. That little compromise hurts your personal testimony for Christ.

Jesus called out the church in Thyatira because they tolerated believers who compromised faithful living in order to get along with

---
[1] Vs. 26

culture. A true believer doesn't compromise. He stands firm to the end. No compromise is too little to care about.

3:1–6

Sardis was a city whose citizens prided themselves on being the safest city in Asia. Standing fifteen hundred feet above the valley floor, the sides of which ridge were smooth and precipitous, the only easy approach was along a spur that connected with Mt. Tmolus. Sardis was a very wealthy city because of the gold found in the river below. The splendor, the wealth, the magnificence, and the luxury of Sardis were the seeds of their downfall. They grew soft and flabby.

Croesus, King of Sardis went to war with Cyrus of Persia somewhere around 549 BC.[1] Cyrus laid siege to the city but could not get in. After 14 days he offered a reward to anyone who could find a way into the city. A soldier named Hyeroeades was watching the battlements when he noticed a Sardian soldier drop his helmet and then make his way down to retrieve it. He knew there must be a crack in the rock. That night he led an assault up through the fault and found the battlements completely unguarded. The people of Sardis were so confident in their safety they were all sleeping, and so Sardis fell to Cyrus. The Christian church in Sardis was quite like the city itself.

Jesus identified Himself as the one who holds the seven Spirits of God and the seven stars. The seven Spirits were already mentioned. It goes back to Isaiah 11:2 and denotes the complete ministry of the Holy Spirit. The seven stars represent the seven churches, which are the possession of Christ. People often confuse the nature of the church, acting as if it belongs to us and we have a right to administer and govern the church to suit ourselves and our own purposes. In fact, every church belongs to Jesus and decisions regarding the church must be aligned with what Jesus wishes.

Jesus said, I know what your church is all about, the religious stuff you do. I know you have a great reputation, but in reality you're the walking dead. He wasn't being critical of their works. His judgment was against the fact that their activity was for the sake of activity and not for the purpose of helping people know and grow in Christ. They were proud and arrogant just like Sardis had been in 549

---
[1] Cyrus was the king who allowed exiled Jews to return to their homeland. 2 Chr 36:22; Ezra 1:8; 5; and accepted the Lord Isa 44:28; 45:13.

BC. They were confident that they did everything right. Other people talked about how great a church they were. Some churches in America are struggling with this today. Some have become very good at marketing and using techniques and programs to fill the seats in the sanctuary, but are failing to really change the hearts of people. They are growing large crowds of very shallow Christians. It's not that there's something wrong with activities and programs. The problem is that, after all the activity, people are still spiritually dead.[1] If your religion doesn't change your behavior you are the walking dead.

The church at Sardis wasn't troubled by heresy as some of the others were. There is no mention of false teachings, and neither is there talk of attack from outside. Nothing is said of attacks by government authorities or persecution. He doesn't say that the Jews were slandering them. Because there was no Christian life in the church at Sardis it just didn't matter to those who hate Christ. It wasn't worth Satan's attacks. Paul describes Christians who have drifted away from real godliness, who have a form of Christianity but with no power.[2] That's the church at Sardis. It was a church that had lost its vital force, the power of God. It didn't need Satan to stop its influence. They had stopped it themselves. In contrast, a church that is alive, a church that's growing followers of Jesus who live for and like Him, will always be under attack. We can always know when we're doing church right because Satan will come after us. He doesn't want us to successfully help people in their Christian walk.

The church at Sardis had become the walking dead, and so Jesus said, Watch Out! Be continually alert, not sleeping like your city guards 650 years ago. Paul used that same word for the same purpose in 1 Cor 16:13 as did Peter in 1 Pet 5:8. The city of Sardis had its own example of what happens when they don't maintain vigilant discipline. What happened when Cyrus had laid siege to the city happened again about 250 years later. Christians are under constant attack from an enemy whose desire is to keep us out of heaven. Jesus warned of His surprise return several times.[3] Paul also again in 1 Thessalonians 5:6 and as well when encouraging the Elders of the church at Ephesus.[4]

---

[1] Several times in the New Testament dead is used as a metaphor for sin. 1 Tim 5:6; Luke 15:24; Rom 6:13; Eph 2:1
[2] 2 Tim 3:5
[3] Matt 24:42; 26:41; Mark 13:37
[4] Acts 20:29–31a

All was not lost at Sardis. Jesus told them they could strengthen the things that remain. Strengthen means to reinforce something so that it stands upright and strong. It's like a landscaper adding support for a newly planted tree to keep it from falling over until it grows roots sufficient to keep it upright. The citizens of Sardis thought their city was impregnable so they didn't bother reinforcing the defenses even while under siege. Christians should strengthen faith so that it will stand firm no matter what life brings.

Jesus issued a rather serious indictment on that church. What you're doing isn't enough. They did a lot of works, they had activities, worshiped, obeyed customs and observed traditions, but none of that resulted in changed lives. It was all empty before God. They were the walking dead.

Jesus outlined three actions we should take if we find ourselves among the walking dead. One, keep on remembering every day what we have received and heard. Never forget the message of Christ we heard when we accepted Him. New Christians haven't forgotten how life changed. They tend to be excited and enthusiastic. They want to learn and to serve. Often, after a while, many Christians sort of lose that excitement and enthusiasm. They still believe and love Jesus, but they grow soft and lethargic in their faith. They don't really listen to sermons. They endure them. They don't feel the need to be in the Word. They're satisfied being connected to a church even if they're not very active themselves. Jesus says, remember how you used to be and what you promised to be in Christ.

Two, obey. We need to be serious about obeying the Word and will of God. Christians who walk with Christ one day and walk without Him the next are among the walking dead. Too many are capable of great nobility one minute and great disloyalty the next. Too many are capable of sacrificial kindness in one instance and brutal selfishness the next. The command of Jesus is that we would constantly and continually obey His will.

Third, repent. As we said before, repentance is not penance. Penance is paying the price. In this case it is a price that Jesus has already paid. Repentance is changed behavior, a decisive action when we put away the old man and put on the new. These actions are encompassed in the warning, Watch out! You don't know when I'll come. I'll surprise you like a sneak thief. They knew from their history what it means to have someone come like a thief. This warning is valid for all Christians. We don't know when Jesus will return. Even when we're done studying The Revelation we still won't know when He will return. But He will come. It may be a thousand years, or it may be today. Don't let any teacher tell you that Jesus can't come back until certain things happen. He'll come back when God says it's time, just like He first came when God said the time was right.

There was a ray of hope that shone through in Sardis. There were a few in that church who had remained faithful. They're described as Christians who haven't soiled their clothes. In most pagan religion no worshiper was allowed to approach a temple of a god in unclean clothes. For them relationship to god was an external thing, whereas for the Christian it describes the one who keeps his soul clean. In baptism a man promises to God that he'll live for Christ. In those days a new Christian was sometimes given a new white robe when he was baptized, symbolic of the cleansing of his life. Those who have not soiled their clothes will walk with Jesus dressed in white.

In the Persian court (remember the Persians ruled Sardis after Cyrus defeated them) the king's trusted favorites were given the privilege of walking in the royal garden with the king. They were called the Companions of the Garden. Those who remain faithful to God will gain the privilege of walking with God like Enoch who walked with God.[1] He had walked with God on earth and then he walked with God in heaven. The Christian who walks with God on earth is promised to walk with Him in heaven also.

As in previous letters, Jesus offered some promises to those who continually overcome. They'll be dressed in white. White stands for victory, festivity, purity, and perfection. Also their names will never be blotted out of the book of life (which assumes that their names were at least at one time written in the book of life).[2] When someone dies his name is erased from the roles of active members of clubs and organizations. The one who is continually overcoming never has to worry about his name being erased from the book of life. Jesus will confess the names of those who are continually overcoming before God. He had said that whoever acknowledges Him before men He will acknowledge before God.[3] Jesus is forever true to

---

[1] Gen 5:24

[2] Gen 32:32f; Ps 69:28; Dan 12:1; Phil 4:3

[3] Jesus used the same word as in Matt 10:32f.

whoever is true to Him. He makes no such promise to who is unfaithful and doesn't remain firm to the end.

3:7–13

Habitat for Humanity originated from Koinonia Farm in Americus, GA, created by Clarence Jordan, a man with two earned PH. D. degrees, one in agriculture and one in Greek and Hebrew in the 1940's. As an African American he experienced heavy resistance, much of it from church people. Eventually the KKK came with guns and torches burning every building on the farm except for Jordan's house which they riddled with bullets. All but Jordan and one other black family fled. A reporter came to the farm and found Jordan working in a field. I heard the awful news. You've put 14 years into this farm. There's nothing left. Just how successful do you think you've been? Jordan answered, About as successful as the cross. Sir, I don't think you understand us. What we're about is not success, but faithfulness. In each of the previous letters Jesus had a rebuke for the congregation. This letter is the only one without such a rebuke. Instead Jesus praised them for their faithfulness.

Philadelphia was a center for the spread of Greek culture and language. When the Muslims invaded the region, only Philadelphia resisted and remained a Greek city until the 14th century. They were also the last remnant of Christianity and still today they have a Christian church.

Jesus identified Himself as the one who is Holy and true (genuine God as opposed to false gods) and the one who holds the key of David. This is an obscure reference. A key is a symbol of authority.[1] Jesus was claiming the authority to allow access to God. What He keeps opening no one will close and what He keeps closing no one can open. Only Jesus can open the door to God. He gave the Christians of Philadelphia an open door.

In 17 AD there was a terrible earthquake with tremors continuing for years. People were constantly running out of the city to escape the destruction. They certainly understood what it means to enjoy an open door.

A good explanation for the open door is that it is a missionary opportunity. Philadelphia was a missionary outpost for Greek

---
[1] Isa 22:22

culture. Paul referred to his opportunities with the Gospel as an open door.[1] Jesus referred to Himself as the door to salvation.[2] Philadelphia was such an opportunity for the Christian Gospel.

Jesus praised this apparently small and weak church that people didn't gush about. I know you're weak but you have obeyed My Word and held my name. Not just did they keep His word, they kept on keeping His Word. It wasn't a one and done thing. They continually kept His word in spite of the pressure from the Greeks and Jews. When their culture was telling them that belief in Jesus was unnecessary and even bigoted, they still wouldn't deny what Jesus stood for. As a reward for their faithfulness Jesus made some promises. He said, I'll make this synagogue of Satan, fake Jews, liars, bow at your feet and admit that I have loved you. God had made a similar promise to Israel but the Jewish nation had lost its place in the plan of God.[3] The promises of Israel have been inherited by the church of Christ, so Jesus promised to the church in Philadelphia that the synagogue of Satan, Jews who didn't believe Jesus, will bow before them.

He promised that they'll be spared the persecution that is still coming. Because they patiently obeyed He said He would protect them from suffering that tests others. Many others were going to be tested. Some will pass the test and some will fail. These people had already proven themselves to be faithful. There was no need for further testing.

As He closed the letter Jesus reminded them, I am coming again, so hold on. This serves as both a warning and a source of comfort. The Bible is clear that whoever does not know God and obey the Gospel will be punished.[4] One purpose for holding on is to keep the crown they have won. Right now they have a crown of righteousness that no one can take away from a faithful believer. But God may take it away from the unfaithful and give it to someone else.[5]

Jesus used two more images of victory. He said that they will be pillars of God's Temple. A pillar is vital to the structure of a temple.

---

[1] 1 Cor 16:8; 2 Cor 2:12; Col 4:3; Acts 14:27

[2] John 10:9

[3] Isa 60:14; 45:14, 49:23

[4] 2 Thess 1:8

[5] There are numerous examples in the Bible of people who have surrendered their calling which was then given to another: Esau gave up his place as first born to Jacob; Reuben gave up his role as leading brother to Judah; Saul gave up his kingship to David; Judas gave up his place as an Apostle to Matthias; Jews gave up their status as the people of God to Gentiles.

This is an image of security for the one continually overcoming. He also said that He would mark them as part of the Kingdom of God.

The city of Philadelphia didn't have that security. After the earthquake Tiberius gave generously to rebuild the city so in gratitude the name was changed to Neocaesarea. Later it was changed to Flavia in honor of the family name of Vespasian. Neither of those names lasted long as it was changed again to Philadelphia.

3:14–22

It takes energy to do some things. Doing nothing requires no expense, and for some Christians that's what they do, nothing. They don't take risks because it's safer to do nothing. They're not moved by the plight of other people because, having been hurt, they're afraid to try again. Martin Luther said the most dangerous trial of all is when there is no trial and everything goes well, for then a man is tempted to forget God.

Can you believe some Christians would forget God even as they go to church and put money in the offering plate and sing worship songs and shake everybody's hand afterward? I doubt they actually forget God. They just become indifferent to the things of God. Everything is going well in life so they don't feel the need to be very concerned. I suspect it happens more often than we'd like to admit. Some Christians have it all together. They have few if any problems. Life is good. They believe in Jesus but with no challenges, they've grown complacent.

The Christians in Laodicea were just such people. As we listen to the letter, notice that as the letter to the church in Philadelphia included no rebuke, this one includes no praise.

Laodicea was named by Antiochus after his wife Laodice. Located on the main road between Ephesus and Syria it was among the wealthiest cites of the world. When an earthquake destroyed the city in 61 AD they declined any help from Rome to rebuild. They had plenty of wealth which they saw as a sign of God's favor. They were the epitome of a neutral city. They didn't build any kind of fortification because any enemy could just surround the city, cut off the water supply which came by aqueduct from six miles away, and wait for them to surrender when they got thirsty.

They mass produced garments made from the luxurious black

wool of the sheep raised in the surrounding fields. They had an early eye and ear clinic where they produced medicine that they sold around the world. Apparently the good church people of Laodicea had adopted the attitude of the city. They had become intoxicated by how good life was. They didn't need to be like the man in the parable who stood far off from the altar and wouldn't even lift his head but said, God have mercy on me, a sinner.[1] Why would they? God was obviously blessing them and He wouldn't do that if they were bad.

Jesus identified Himself with three designations. The Amen, the final word on truth. (Remember how Jesus would begin a teaching, I tell you the truth? That's Amen.) The faithful and true witness. There are three conditions for one who would be a faithful and true witness. He must be an eyewitness. He must be honest and he must be able to tell. That's Jesus. The ruler of God's creation. Your text might read "the beginning." The word used here can be translated ruler, head, or source. The use of the dative pronoun suggest translating it ruler.

I know you, Jesus said, I know your deeds, that you're not cold and you're not hot. I wish you were one or the other. You're lukewarm. Nobody asks for a lukewarm cup of coffee or soaks aching muscles in a lukewarm tub. I wish you were cold or hot. Instead you are lukewarm. Lukewarm Christians are people who try to be neutral. They don't want to make waves. Since they're not being hassled and life is going well they're satisfied that God must favor them. They're half–hearted about living the Christian life. They're ready to compromise. They're indifferent, unwilling to take a stand. They're really not good for much when you think about it. A.T. Robertson wrote, There is no real Christianity without enthusiasm.

Jesus doesn't see much value in lukewarm Christians. Lukewarm Christians aren't salt and they're not light. They're Christian as long as it doesn't interfere with daily living. He has an interesting way of expressing what He thinks of them: You make me sick! His actual words are, I am about to puke you out of my mouth. You know that feeling when you're about to throw up. That's what Jesus feels about lukewarm Christians. Imagine if we had one of our missionaries as guest preacher and he stood up and said, Church, you've been dropping big checks on our mission for many years and we thank you, but you make me want to throw up.

---

[1] Luke 18:13

It's interesting that Jesus wasn't grieved at them, or angry. He was disgusted! Their religion was shameful, hypocritical. Y'all think you're rich (OK, He didn't say y'all.) You think you're rich, that you don't need anything from anybody, not from Rome, not from God. You don't even know. You're wretched, pitiful, poor, blind, and naked.

Well thanks for the compliment. His description of them negates all of their pride in themselves. They were wretched but they thought everyone was jealous of their affluence. They didn't think of themselves as pitiful. Who is to be more pitied than the one who thinks all is well when actually he's very sick? They thought they were rich. They had more money than Notre Dame but you can't buy eternal life. They had the eye clinic but they were spiritually blind. They made the finest tunics in the known world, but fashionable clothing doesn't cover guilt. They thought everything was right in the world but in reality they were dangerously close to hell. Not because they weren't believers. Because they were. But because they were lukewarm believers. They weren't salt, they were just a little bit of sodium chloride. They weren't light, no more than a faint glow.

Because they were lukewarm, Jesus said He didn't have much use for them. They have denied the purpose God had for them. In the Sermon on the Mount Jesus suggested that being lukewarm made them no longer good for anything except to be thrown out and trampled by men.[1] Like a good friend He offered counsel. With all your wealth you're used to buying whatever you need but you buy from the wrong source. Now buy from me.

He mentioned three things to buy, again from their context. Purified gold, stuff of real value. White clothes instead of trusting the security of their tunic factory. And real eye salve, not the limited stuff they could get from their clinic. Salvation must be obtained rightfully. Jesus said, buy from me. How could they buy from Jesus? They had nothing to offer. The 7,500 male Jews who, according to tax records, lived in Laodicea knew how. Come, all you who are thirsty, come to the waters; and you who have no money, come, buy and eat! Come, buy wine and milk without money and without cost.[2]

Lukewarm Christians disgust Jesus but He still loves them. Those whom I love I rebuke and discipline. Usually when Jesus says

---

[1] Matt 5:13
[2] Isa 55:1

He loves He uses the word agape, unselfish love of choice. The word He used here refers to a warm affectionate feeling of love. I really care about you. That's why I rebuke and discipline you. He's not railing or scolding. Rebuke means to compel to see error and admit wrong. Discipline, like a parent, teaches a child how to do something right.

Then he commands them to be zealous, as opposed to indifferent, and to repent. Notice again that this was singular. Each of you, on your own, not as a group thing, stop being lukewarm and get serious.

Behold! He said. I am already standing at the door and I continue to stand. I am continually knocking. Jesus is on the outside but He's the one initiating the contact. He must also be calling out because He said, If anyone hears my voice and opens the door, I will come in and eat with him, and he with me. Again it's singular. If anyone hears, and if that one opens the door, I will enter. An often seen picture of Jesus shows Him knocking on a door, not pounding. There is no knob on the outside. The one on the inside must open for Him.

If anyone will open the door for Him He will enter and they will dine together. The word dine is the word for supper, the meal where we sit and talk and share our days and talk about tomorrow, where the kids talk about school, and mom and dad talk about work, and everybody talks about the great show they watched on TV last night. This is fellowship and sharing. Jesus will descend the throne of Heaven and fellowship with the one who opens the door of his heart to Him. Jesus said, If anyone loves me, he will obey my teaching. My father will love him, and we will come to him and make our home with him.[1]

To the one continually overcoming I will give the right to sit with me on my throne just as I overcame and sat down with my Father on His throne. Who gets to sit on the throne with Jesus? According to Jesus, Not everyone who says Lord! Lord! Will enter the kingdom of Heaven.[2] He goes on to say that many will claim to have done lots of religious stuff in His name but He will say to them, I never knew you. Get away from me, you evildoers.[3]

---

[1] John 14:23
[2] Matt 7:21
[3] Matt 7:23

He who has an ear, let him hear what the Spirit says to the churches. Are your ears hearing the Spirit's message? This is tough to think about. I don't want to teach this message. This may be the scariest teaching in the Bible for Christians. We're assured that nothing can separate us from the love of God, yet in this text we hear Jesus say, I'm about to puke you out of my mouth. What do you think it means to be puked out of Jesus' mouth? Does that sound like, Well done good and faithful servant? William Barclay wrote, Hard as it may sound, the meaning of this terrible threat of the Risen Christ is that it is better not even to start on the Christian way than it is to start and then slip and drift into conventional and meaningless Christianity of respectability.[1] Lukewarm Christianity is worse than no Christianity.

Francis Chan has a harsh assessment of lukewarm Christians. Lukewarm is not Christian. Lukewarm is wretched, pitiful, poor, blind, and naked. There's an old expression about someone who runs around like a chicken with its head cut off. I've seen it and it really is amazing. The chicken is dead but she doesn't know it and literally runs around the barnyard. Lukewarm Christians don't know they're dead, so they run around the church as if everything is fine. If you're lukewarm, you're dead, but you probably don't know it.

Jesus doesn't like lukewarm churches, or Christians (if there is such a thing). What is lukewarm?[2] This is uncomfortable teaching but it is Jesus talking. If a Christian church has lost its first love and doesn't repent He says, I'll take away your status as a church. If you allow anything else my place as the God of your life and don't repent, I'll fight against you when I return. If you compromise Christian living in order to get along with the culture and don't repent, I will see to it that you suffer the second death. If you're religious but are not alive and don't repent, I'll come back and you'll have to answer to me."

PART TWO: 4:1–8:5

The bulk of what creates confusion among modern readers is chapters 4–22. The Revelation can be seen as two divisions. The first is chapters 1 through 11 and the second is chapters 12 through 22. The first division describes the struggle of Christ (Team Jesus)

---

[1] Barclay, Revelation p.180
[2] See appendix A for a list Francis Chan put together of descriptors of lukewarm people.

against all evil under the leadership of Satan (Team Satan) emphasizing the victory of Christ. The second division describes the antagonists (main evil characters) who will harass the church. In this we see how Satan prosecutes his war with God.

We've already begun looking at the first division where Jesus is identified for who He is in all His glory and majesty. His relationship with the church is seen in seven letters He dictated to seven specific churches.

The next movement of the first division begins with John looking into the throne room of Heaven. Keep in mind that this is a vision. He is for a moment not in the Spirit for he has been listening to Jesus dictate letters to the churches. As Jesus speaks to him he immediately returns to the state of being in direct spiritual contact with Jesus, wide awake to receive communication from God. Beginning in chapter 4 verse 2 John "sees" God's plan for history written on a scroll that has been sealed with seven seals. As the Lamb of God opens the scroll John sees a historical battle between God (Team Jesus) and evil (Team Satan) unfold. The calamities described are God's hand active in history including what we would see as natural occurrences. He does not see physical beings with his physical eyes. They're symbols of the reality of the cosmic battle.

4:1–3

Having listened to and written Jesus' letters to the churches John returns once again to his vision. He saw an open door into Heaven. The voice of Christ calls out to him again telling him that what he is about to see is what will happen throughout history until Jesus returns. It is not the physical, material world he will see but the spiritual reality of the great battle.

He sees the throne room of Heaven.[1] A throne has the purpose of seating He who governs all of reality. This should comfort the readers to be reminded that God governs all things including trial and blessing. Sitting on the throne is God, described in beauty and majesty. This is not a picture of God as if He could be captured in an image.

---

[1] "Throne" is used 17 times in chapters four and five.

4:4–6a

Now about the twenty–four elders around God representing the old and new covenants (Israel and the church). They wear the clothes of purity and wreaths of victory. Lightning and thunder are seen and heard because God speaks with power and authority. John sees seven lamps which are the seven spirits (the Holy Spirit in His fullness). He sees not a sea of glass but something beyond description that looked like a sea of glass.

4:6b–11

Also around the throne are four living ones.[1] They stand like security guards for God.[2] They look "like" a lion, an ox, a man, and an eagle. The lion represents strength, the ox service, the man intelligence, and the eagle swiftness. Their presence enhances the significance of the throne. Everything is arranged around the throne focused in reverence, humility and awe on the One sitting on the throne. So great is the throne of God that they are constantly in worship. The Lord Reigns! (19:6) Jesus understands that if we recognize what it means that everything surrenders to His will one way or the other, we can know comfort in the midst of trials.

5:1–5

God held a scroll (book) that had within it His eternal plan. It had been sealed with seven seals so that no one could know what is written within. Whoever can break the seals to open the scroll carries out God's plan. On Earth no one was worthy to open the scroll. How will God's purpose be completed if no one opens the scroll? One of the Elders points out that the Lion of Judah, the Root of David has triumphed. Certainly this speaks of Jesus the Messiah. He has won victory over sin, the obstacle that interrupted God's plan, thus He is able to carry out God's plan.

5:6–14

When Jesus takes hold of the scroll the living creatures and the Elders begin to worship. Adoration and praise break out because Jesus accepts the responsibility of being King of Kings.

---

[1] They are probably cherubim mentioned in Ezk 10.
[2] Gen 3:24

Uncountable numbers of angels break into song, the entire creation is ruled by one throne. Ultimately all things must glorify Him. The Lord reigns!

As the scroll is read history is happening. We'll see that we live in a fallen world and there will be persecution. There will also be natural disasters, car wrecks, wars, and cancer. Because sin entered the world people will do sinful things and sin always leads to death. There is a lot of ugly in the chapters to come. We should remember this when trials come. We live by faith not by sight because in the midst of suffering it is extremely difficult to see anything other than the immediate experience. It's all within God's plan and rule. We can rejoice knowing that with Jesus we will survive. That's why we worship Him. Now Jesus opens the seals one at a time. As each one opens John sees persecution of the church (great tribulation) and punishment for evil.

6:1–2

The first seal reveals a rider on a white horse. The rider symbolizes Jesus (19:11). He was given a wreath, a symbol of victory. Jesus is elsewhere identified as "the conqueror."[1] The next three riders are subservient to the Christ, refining and strengthening God's people. Each comes with dreadful power. They are Christ's instruments for refining and strengthening His people. What Satan intends as a means to exterminate God's people, Jesus uses to make us strong.

Three things are important for understanding the symbolism. First, this isn't allegory. All the parts do not represent some specific event or player. They make a general statement, there will be killing, famine, war, catastrophe, etc. Second, we must be careful not to attach too much significance to numbers. For example one third simply means "some" not an exact amount. Third, whenever the white horse appears, the red horse of persecution follows. Jesus is always followed by persecution directed by Satan.

6:3–8

Opening the seals reveals the calamities of history. They are not intended to identify an exact reference, rather they serve as a

---
[1] Rev 3:21; 5:5; John 16:31

warning; before Jesus returns things will go from bad to worse so we must be vigilant to remain faithful.

As the first rider symbolizes strength, the second symbolizes terror, the third warfare, and the fourth conquest. The rider on the red horse indicates religious persecution. He has power to cause men to slaughter one another. The word slay or slaughter is used in 1 John 3:12 of Cain murdering Abel. In The Revelation John used this word eight times, all but one referring to the execution of Christ or God's people (5:6, 9; 13:8; 18:24). The rider holds a sword, a sacrificial knife or a weapon for killing.

The third rider atop a black horse brings oppression. The imagery is of the rich enjoying expensive food while the poor suffer injustice. A man (of faith in Christ) is unable to support his family. He will be forced to work on the Lord's Day to provide. He has no place in society unless he agrees with the culture.

The fourth horse is a sickly color of puss indicating death and disease. Death and Hades are mentioned with limited power to kill by the sword, famine, pestilence, beasts. These affect all mankind, not just Christians.

6:9–11

Opening the fifth seal gives John a vision of the souls of Christians who gave their lives in Jesus' name. They had been slaughtered and were crying out for vengeance. Two great questions are asked. How long must we wait and who can stand? The world is full of terrible evil and faithful Christians struggle with the unfairness of it. The Revelation tells us that God loves us and He hears our cries. He has done something about it but we must wait for His timing. This should resonate with today's believers because we realize that, while God doesn't explain suffering, He surrounds it and gives us the strength to stand.

They are encouraged to wait patiently because the time is not yet. In the meantime they are given white robes, symbolic of righteousness and holiness, assuring them that their prayers have been heard but the time set by God is not complete.

6:12–17

When the sixth seal is opened the end is revealed. It's the Day of Judgment, the catastrophic end of time symbolized by six objects of terror. An earthquake, the sun turning black, the moon appearing as blood (symbols of judgment), stars falling, the sky rolling up, and mountains and islands being removed from their places are God's final and complete wrath on those who have persecuted His people. These images cannot be reality (a star couldn't fall to the earth for the earth is too small) but rather are symbolic of God's judgment on evil.

Terror falls on six classes of people; kings, princes, officers, rich, strong, slave, and free. No one is exempt. Everyone who does not believe Jesus is seized with fear and run to escape judgment but there is nowhere to hide. It's over!

Before the seventh seal is opened John writes an interlude emphasizing God's ownership and protection of His people.

7:1–4

The four angels control the agencies of destruction. A fifth angel has the seal of the living God, ready to mark those who will be saved from the judgment because they remained faithful to Christ.

This seal does three things: it protects, marks ownership, and certifies genuineness. The seal is the name of the Lamb (22:4) and those who receive it are those whose names are written in the Book of Life, numbering 144,000. Remember, numbers are symbolic and do not indicate an exact number. They represent all believers of all time.

The list in verses 5–8 could give the impression that the saved are all of Israel, equally distributed among the 12 tribes. That would violate what we have already established, that true Israel is all who believe God. Regardless of ethnicity, it is he who overcomes who will inherit God's promises. The point of The Revelation is that those who remain faithful to the end, enduring and resisting government persecution, cultural seduction, and false teaching, will be saved.[1]

---

[1] Jesus said in Matt 24:10 & 13...many will turn away from the faith...but he who stands firm to the end will be saved.

7:5–8

John next saw a multitude of people too large to count from every location, race, and language, as well as the angels around the throne and the four living creatures (4:6b) standing in God's presence to worship. They were dressed in the white robes of purity and waving palm branches reminiscent of the pilgrims on Palm Sunday. This represents the church at worship in triumph.

7:9–17

The Elder questioning John wasn't looking for information. He knows. He's focusing attention on worshiping sinners, now righteous. The worshipers John sees are all who have faithfully endured persecution and trouble on earth, who have denied cultural seduction, and who have resisted false teaching. It's a glorious picture of life eternal in Heaven where they (Team Jesus) never again will be hassled by the enemies of God (Team Satan). Just as the Good Shepherd of Psalm 23 Jesus will protect and serve them.

8:1–5

This part of The Revelation ends with the opening of the seventh seal making way for the troubles that will affect the earth, including the church throughout the millennium. The troubles described herein are God's retribution to Team Satan, warning and punishment for opposing Jesus Christ and His faithful. It is so serious everyone is stunned to silence. There is no arguing. There is silence as Habakkuk wrote, The Lord is in His Holy Temple. Let all the earth be silent before Him.[1] He has gotten everyone's attention.

An angel filled an incense pot, representing Jesus interceding on behalf of believers. In Old Testament worship incense accompanied prayer. God hears our prayers. After burning the incense the angel filled the censer with fire and cast it on the earth spilling many seemingly natural troubles. Judgment begins! Trouble is not a single event. It's all the trouble on earth. Keep in mind that the trumpets are not separate from the seals as if they are new events.

---

[1] Heb 2:20

PART THREE: 8:6–11:19

This part describes evil and the punishment for sin with ugly images.

8:6–7

God unleashes His action causing disasters on earth. This makes me wonder how much of God's goodness are we missing today because of evil in the world. Some of the trouble affects the faithful along with the evil. Before "The Fall" (Genesis 3) the world God had created was a place of goodness and peace. Now there is trouble. Why does God allow suffering? He allows suffering as punishment for sin, to discipline His followers, and to strengthen them to stand.

8:8–9

The terror of God's judgment affects even the land and the seas. These are truly awe–inspiring troubles. The destructive force of natural disasters continually awes viewers as it is shown on media.

8:10–11

Trouble also befalls inland water ways. There is nowhere for evil to find sanctuary. Could the bitter effects of floods and the like be God's punishment? Wormwood is a general name for the class of plants known as artemisis characterized by bitter taste.[1] The name is associated with the sin of idolatry (Deut 29:17f).

8:12

The sun, moon, and stars are vitally important for life on earth. Trouble there is trouble on earth. For example, the power of a sun spot messes with our electronic media. It's all controlled by God

8:13

The vision is interrupted by the sight of a soaring eagle. The eagle speaks loudly for all to hear. Four trumpets have sounded. The next three will be worse, but to whom?

---

[1] Barclay, Vol. 2 p,54

9:1–6

Satan has lost his position and place in Heaven. John had personally heard Jesus say that He saw Satan fall.[1] Satan, the star, is able to access The Abyss. The Abyss is a place of confinement for spirits.[2] (In Luke 8:31 a demon whom Jesus confronted begged Jesus not to order him into the abyss.) Opening the Abyss releases a cloud of ugly and evil deception. The evil is not from God but from Satan. God allows it because He uses even evil to punish and warn. Grotesquely and hellishly described locusts appear out of the cloud. They have the power and influence of hell on earth in the hearts of men, however they are limited. They cannot kill men but they are able to create havoc, taking away what is good and holy.[3]

9:7–11

The horse–like locusts are dressed for battle. This is a terrifying picture of the power of evil led by their king, Satan. It's all Satan's work!

9:12–19

The river Euphrates (Assyria, Babylon) represents the evil world. The four angels here are not the ones of 7:1. These are evil beings who cause war between men. The sixth trumpet is not about a particular war. The images indicate the engines of war. Note the description of riders with breastplates colored to look like a deadly inferno, and their mounts belching fire and brimstone. The point is that in the judgment, according to God's plan the one who reigns will punish the wicked with disasters of every kind, even some not known to men at that time. We should take note that the number of evil men and angels is astronomical. This should serve as a warning. God will punish evil men.

9:20–21

Sadly, God's warnings go unheeded. To the point of stubbornness many refuse to repent, instead they continue in sin.

---

[1] Luke 10:18
[2] Leon Morris, p. 156
[3] Isa 5:20. Woe to those who call evil good and good evil, who put darkness for light and light for darkness, who put bitter for sweet and sweet for bitter.

Their refusal to believe God results in the pouring out of bowls of wrath and the final judgment.

10:1–4

We meet still another angel. This one is closely associated with Jesus and is described in hyperbolic images.[1] His appearance suggests holiness and authority, and his message concerns every created thing. We're never told what the seven thunders said. It is part of the mystery of God. There are things He has set in motion that we don't know and probably never will.[2] This angel is not Jesus. Jesus is not an angel nor is He called one.

10:5–7

His message is simple: when God's time is complete there will be no more delay, the final act happens. The word "accomplished" is the same word John quoted Jesus saying It is finished.[3] The final act comes with the seventh trumpet in 11:15–19.

Just as following the opening of the sixth seal, there is an interlude (10:8–11:14) following the sounding of the sixth trumpet (Ch. 7).

10:8–11

John is told to take the little scroll from the hand of the angel and eat it. The sweet tasting scroll turns to sourness in his stomach.[4] The Gospel is sweet but always followed by bitter persecution. Lessons from God are sweet even if they are difficult to swallow.

11:1–6

John is told to measure the Temple but not the outer court. The Temple is the sanctuary of God, the true people of God, those who remain faithful to believe and obey Jesus. All others are excluded. Faithful believers will suffer at the hands of those on the outside but will not perish because they're in the Temple. No such promise is

---

[1] Compare the image of Jesus in 1:7, 13–15
[2] People who wish to use the Revelation to predict the future should be careful. We don't have all the information. It's like doing math without all the factors. e.g. 7+4+3+? = ?
[3] John 19:30
[4] The scroll reminds of Ezk 2:9 and Ps 119:103

offered for those on the outside.[1] They will suffer the judgment.

Persecution of the faithful is not unlimited. No one knows exactly what 42 months and 1,260 days represents other than that it describes the present age when believers are subject to the pressures of persecution, cultural seduction, and false teaching.

Two witnesses, called olive trees and lampstands, will testify of Christ for this limited time. They "prophesy" not to tell fortunes but to proclaim the name of Jesus. These represent the church in witness to Christ. Olive trees produce oil for the lamps which we already have learned represent the church who are the light of the world.[2] Hendriksen sees the two witnesses to be the preaching and the observance of sacraments by the church.[3] Their witness condemns evil on the basis of the Word of God, justifying judgment against whoever rejects their message. Judgment is poured out on whoever harms the witnesses. The church continues this witness today.

11:7–10

When the witnesses are through, the beast we will read about in Ch. 13 will rise up and kill them. Not all believers will be killed at the hands of evil. There will be faithful believers still living when Christ returns. We're not told how we'll know that our witness is finished, but when God decides, it's over.

Two enemies of God's people (Egypt and Sodom), prodded by Satan, represent the immoral and anti–Christian world. The church is silenced; seemingly dead and no longer effective. This is the battle of Armageddon. The world will smugly celebrate victory of evil over righteousness, sending gifts and gloating. The truth of God's Word will no longer affect them. Evil thinks it has won, but we read on.

11:11–12

God will resurrect His church. Evil will see that it is defeated. God will demonstrate His power.

---

[1] Matthew 7:22f
[2] Matt 5:14ff
[3] Hendriksen, p. 144f

11:13–14

Destruction begins. The church is taken to heaven while evil men get what's coming to them. Seeing what they missed, men will be terrified. They will give glory to God but not in praise. It will be more like Pharaoh and Nebuchadnezzar who acknowledged God's supremacy only after being defeated but not loving and worshiping Him. That's the end of their punishment on earth, but something worse is coming.

11:15–19

The seventh angel sounds his trumpet introducing (not describing) the final judgment.

Living beings begin to declare that God reigns eternally. Angels sing. The Elders, representing all who believe God, bow in worship and praise. Jesus is called the one who is and who was. He's not called the one who is to come because at this point He is here. God's sovereignty is revealed absolutely and clearly. John is given a look inside the sanctuary of Heaven to see the Ark of the Covenant, symbolic of intimate fellowship of God and His people.

This part of The Revelation teaches us to sing during our trials because God is in control. Everything is just as He knew. God took the risk of freewill but resulted in evil in the world. Some choose to obey and some choose to rebel. The message is that we will be hurt in many ways none–the–less we know that God loves us and will avenge our pain. When it's all over, we who remain faithful will enjoy the eternal heaven.

PART FOUR: CH. 12–14:20

While parts One, Two, and Three (the first 11 chapters) describe the outward struggle between the church and the world, parts Four through Seven (chapters 12–20) picture the background of this struggle. Satan doesn't simply find a home on earth. He's actively engaged in luring people away from God, deceiving them to doubt God's goodness, and from their own minds to think that ugly is beautiful and beautiful is ugly.

Jesus warned of this when He said, False Christs will appear and perform great signs and miracles to deceive even the elect.[1] Satan is

[1] Matt 24:24

called the great deceiver who masquerades as an angel of light[1] and the father of lies, whose native tongue is lying.[2] Is there a better way to deceive than to get people to redefine good and evil? Consider how today that which is sinful is redefined to be acceptable.

Part Four introduces the dragon, two beasts, and a woman (the church). As with each of the parts we return to the beginning, the first coming of Christ, and each ends with reference to the judgment in 14:14ff.

12:1–6

A woman is described with beautiful imagery. She is the church (all who believe Jesus), the people of God who oppose the devil. On earth we see the faults of the church but God has endowed her with splendor and glory. In contrast to the woman, evil is personified as a violent dragon and two grotesque beasts. Ugly images expose evil for what it is. The world is a battleground in which we must fight. It is not a playground in which we amuse ourselves. Evil has power, but limited power. This vision is meant to help us see evil more clearly. Phony religion and godless governments are not innocent well-meaning but misguided institutions. They're grotesque beasts that serve the dragon. The dragon has seven heads (dominion in the world) with seven crowns (diadems of power, not wreaths of victory) and ten horns (destructive power).

The woman is pregnant as it is the church's task to bring forth the Messiah, the Savior of mankind. The dragon is poised to kill her child as soon as He is born. John sees the child as the one who will rule all peoples and will defeat Satan. The dragon will try but fail to kill the child. Both the woman and the child are protected by God.[3]

12:7–12

There was a war between Michael the Archangel and his friends (Team Jesus) against Satan and his demonic posse (Team Satan). Both sides fight. However, we should note that Michael attacked

---

[1] 2 Cor 11:14

[2] John 8:44

[3] Hendriksen connects this to Gen. 3:15, "I will put enmity between you and the woman, and between your offspring and hers; he will crush your head, and you will strike his heel." He narrates the activity of Satan through the Old Testament as he seeks to destroy the family from which will come the Savior.

Satan who fought back.[1] Satan lost that war and was hurled down. He lost his place as accuser of the faithful. He can accuse no longer because there is no evidence of sin. Sins have been forgiven.[2] Because Satan's efforts were defeated by Jesus he is filled with fury. He knows that compared to eternity his time is short but he will not give up the fight. He will aim his anger at the church.

12:13–17

Satan is not a gracious loser. Having failed to kill the child he renews his attack on the woman but again she is protected by God. Following that failure he turns his wrath against the church (us). We are in this story, and being so should affect how we read The Revelation. We are currently being hunted by a ferocious dragon.

Some people are not bothered by the presence of evil and apparently don't care what The Revelation describes. In vivid terms we're told that the kingdom of God has come. Salvation is now. The faithful win. Satan is filled with wrath. Throughout history on earth Satan does everything he can to harm God's people, but God always provides a way of escape.[3] The dragon was even more enraged when Jesus chose the cross for us, so he made war against those who obey God.

The church is protected from Satan's deceit, that is, he cannot destroy her even though he can lead some astray. This is the 1000 years of Ch. 20. It's the age when witnesses testify of Christ. It's all the time between the first and second comings of Christ, and it's the period of the anti–Christ. Don't make too much of the time numbers, 1,260 days; a time, times and one half time;[4] 42 months. They're not intended to identify specific time periods.

We next meet two agents of the dragon. One a beast out of the sea and the other a beast out of the land. They are persecutors of the church. Think of this in present tense because it is going on now.

13:1–10

John sees a beast, horrible and disgusting appearing out of the sea. It's described in a way to suggest authority and power (horns and

---

[1] Jesus had said that the defensive gates of hades cannot overcome the church. Matt 16:18
[2] Rom 8:34
[3] 1 Cor 10:13
[4] The math works for "time" to be one year. One year, two years, half year.

crowns) given to it from the dragon. It's swift and fierce (leopard) and powerful, ready to kill (bear). It speaks in a frightening way, like a roaring lion ready to destroy its prey. It speaks blasphemies and proud words, false teaching and world views that are antithetical to God.

The world has fallen to its magic. "They worshiped him" means they chose to follow his way instead of God's way. We should remember that Satan is a created being just like all angels and men. He was bestowed with free–will. Once he chose to compete with God as ruler of all, he wielded his power as a weapon and gave it also to his agents. This is the power of Satan persecuting the church with the intent of causing some to put their hope in something other than God.

Seven heads represents all governments that persecute the church. Certainly the reader would think of Babylon, Assyria, and Rome. While the form of government changes the desire to destroy the church never does.

The beast is mortally wounded but is healed, making him seem undefeatable. John's immediate audience may have thought of Nero who viciously persecuted the church. Nero had been responsible for a great fire that destroyed much of Rome. In order to deflect blame he accused Christians instigating murderous rage. Christians were crucified, some covered in oil, nailed to a post and set aflame like a torch. It seemed Rome was mortally wounded when Nero committed suicide in 68AD, but Domitian brought the evil back to life with another round of persecution so intense it seems to have destroyed the church. God however, has always maintained a remnant of true believers who continue the life of the church. There are two kinds of people in the world: those whose names are written in the book of life, and those who worship the beast. The reader is reminded that surviving the persecution requires patient endurance.

13:11–18

A second beast comes from the earth, one that looks harmless, like a lamb, but it's a deception. It is less ugly but speaks like a dragon. It seems attractive to the world.[1] What he says reveals what he stands for. Where the first beast represented anti–Christian governments that carry out Satan's plan, this one represents anti–Christian

---
[1] Satan made himself appear as an angel of light. 2 Cor 11:14

religions and culture that lures people away from Jesus. False teaching always works hand–in–hand with persecution. This beast leads people to trust their own wisdom and understanding rather than God. They don't recognize the beast for what it is.

The beast commands that every person be given a mark.[1] This isn't an outward mark, like a tattoo. It simply means that some people are known to belong to Satan. Compare 7:3. The people of God have a seal, a symbol of authenticity. The people of Satan have a brand, a mark of ownership like a slave owner might use.

"On the forehead" indicates that Satan has captured the mind. "On the right hand" indicates his influence over behavior. This mark refers to the God–opposing, Christ–rejecting, church–persecuting spirit of the anti–Christ active in the thoughts and deeds of evil people. When given the opportunity, governments will require loyalty to the state over loyalty to God. The penalty for failing to be so loyal is to be cancelled by society.

The number 666 is not a code. No amount of mathematical gymnastics can identify a specific person. Six is one less than seven. Seven is perfection. Six is imperfection. The beast is not a specific person, and it is not a perfect being. 666 suggests failure upon failure.

Chapter 14 can be divided into three parts, the first and third are introduced with "I saw, and behold…" The second with only "I saw."

14:1–5

First John saw the Lamb standing with 144,000 people who wore the seal of God (as opposed to the mark of the beast). The number refers to all who have been and are faithful to believe God. They're singing praise in heaven. Only those who are God's can sing this song, similar to what Paul wrote, I tell you that no one who is speaking by the Spirit of God says, "Jesus be cursed," and no one can say, "Jesus is Lord," except by the Holy Spirit.[2] They were among the first people purchased by the blood of Christ. The beast is no match for the church when she is serving God. The church advanced without political power or influence.

---

[1] A stamp of approval. Some have interpreted the mark to be the symbol of Free Mason; the image on the back of an American dime; even the decision to worship on Sunday instead of Saturday.
[2] 1 Cor 12:3

14:6–13

This periscope sees the harvest of the Earth. There are three angels, each with a warning. The first one calls on the reader to give glory to God because it's time for the judgment. A second declares God's victory over Satan. John writes it as if it already has happened. A third warns those who weren't seeing the danger, people so fascinated by the things of the earth that they failed to recognize the coming judgment. The angel warns, serve Satan and suffer the consequences he suffers, torment of never ending burning with no respite. This is elsewhere referred to as the second death.[1] You cannot pursue sin and go to heaven.

Those who remain faithful, who have obeyed God's commands, are blessed with being in the presence of Jesus, seeing Him exactly as He is. They can now rest from the toil of resisting Satan. Their works go with them.

14:14–20

The vision now depicts the harvest separating winners (Team Jesus) and losers (Team Satan). Those who are not of God suffer the wrath of God. John sees "one like a son of man," Jesus, the ruler of all prepared to harvest from the world those who are His. An angel declares that harvest time has come. John the Baptist had proclaimed that Jesus will harvest those who will be saved.[2]

Two more angels are seen, one charging the other to begin the harvest of those who have followed Satan. They are gathered like grapes and cast into the "winepress of God's wrath."

PART FIVE: 15:1-16:21

Like the opening of the seven seals and the sounding of the seven trumpets, seven bowls of wrath being poured out covers the Christian era, the time between the first and second comings of Christ. This, like the other two series of sevens, ends with the end of the world (6:17; 11:17ff; 16:17–21). John calls these the "last" because in them God's judgment is completed. There is no more

---

[1] 2:11; 20:14; 21:8
[2] Matt 3:12

because evil is totally destroyed.

Throughout history God has acted to call men to repentance and punish evil although His actions do not always bring about the repentance He desires. Too often they do not. What we've seen so far in this vision is partial manifestation of God's judgment. These last plagues are directed against those who have so refused. They wear the mark of the beast. They worship the dragon and his agents. Note that the antagonists are the same as before, the dragon and two beasts representing government sponsored or allowed persecution, cultural seduction, and false teachers. The vision ends just as the previous expressions of judgment. It's the end.

15:1–4

As this vision begins John sees the church victorious over the dragon. They have not fallen to his pressure. They have remained faithful to Jesus. They're now free from evil. These victorious believers are beside a sea that looks like glass and fire. They're singing praise. Specifically John sees that they sing the Song of Moses. Remember when the Israelites passed through the Red Sea on dry ground and the Egyptians were drowned, they stood on the opposite shore and sang praise.[1] The praise here gives glory to God for the victory and His judgment. All people will finally see the righteousness and fairness of God in His judgment. Evil has hardened their hearts against Him. They can blame no one but themselves for their destiny.

15:5–8

The Tabernacle of the Testimony calls to mind Exodus 25:16 & 21. "Put in the ark the Testimony, which I will give you. Place the cover (Mercy seat) on top of the ark and put in the ark the Testimony, which I will give you. I believe this testimony is the ultimate mystery of God's plans, including His righteous judgment.

Seven angels come out dressed in purity and majesty. One of the living creatures (4:6) presents to the angels golden bowls filled with the wrath of God. The glory of God in His holy anger produces smoke that fills the temple. No one is able to enter the temple until the plagues are completed indicating that no none could intercede

---

[1] Ex 14 & 15

for those on whom the plagues fall.

Previous expressions of God's wrath were not complete. Judgement herein described on those who oppose God and will not repent offers no more opportunity to repent. By continually hardening their hearts they put themselves in the hands of an angry God. Some people are beyond salvation. Even God has given up on them.

16:1

The loud voice coming from the temple, presumably either God Himself or one of the living creatures, calls for the angels to pour out the bowls of wrath. Notice that the plagues that come with this wrath are very similar to the plagues with which God punished Egypt for their hard hearts. Notice also that in these God uses the elements of the universe to carry out His wrath. He uses them first to encourage repentance and then to punish.

16:2–11

The descriptions are ugly and awful, cumulative not consecutive. God uses incurable disease, maritime disasters, catastrophes of land–based waters, the sun, and darkness to display His wrath. Darkness is the absence of light suggesting that God will remove His light from their presence. The darkness was poured out on the throne of the beast, government.

The angel proclaimed that in His judgment God is just. He is fair and right. This is the vengeance the souls under the altar called for (6:9; 8:3–5). The altar itself, or perhaps the souls under the altar acknowledged that in all of this God is true and just. The wicked however, will not accept God's judgment but curse Him. Like coyotes in a leg–hold trap they gnaw at their own flesh yet find no relief.

16:12–15

Historically the Euphrates River served to deter the nations from the east (Assyria and Babylon) from attacking God's people. Deterred but did not stop. Drying up the river suggests that the way is prepared for the anti–Christian forces to operate. All the forces of the earth are assembled to attack the church. Evil always eventually leads to opposing righteousness. Out of the mouths of the dragon (Satan) and the beast (government) and the false prophet (false religious teaching) come three unclean spirits. This represents that all hell is breaking loose against God's people. Every evil scheme, plan, idea, and thought is aimed to oppose Christ and His church. This is the Battle of Armageddon (11:17ff; 19:11ff; 20:7ff).[1] Satan, government, and false teaching are all gathered against the church. This is the culmination of Satan's assault on the church. Anti-Christian governments, religions, and philosophies all working against the church.

In giving this vision Jesus compelled Himself to remind that He will show up in an unmistakable way to deliver His people. He encourages the readers to remain faithful, dressed in the white clothes and with riches He gives so that they have nothing for which to be ashamed.

16:17–21

The seventh bowl of wrath depicts terror at the final judgment. When it is poured out on the air it falls on all the earth. God calls out in a loud voice, "It has happened." It's a done deal. This is similar to Jesus saying from the cross, "It is finished." The final judgment is now. Judgment Day has arrived.

Babylon, the representative of all evil, is broken into three parts indicating the government with its persecution, the culture with its seduction, and the false teachers with their perverted theology, are all destroyed. God's judgment comes down from heaven like hailstones destroying everything. Evil men, their hearts hardened by continued evil acts, continue to curse God.

PART SIX: 17:1–19:21

This part of the vision describes the nature and history including the fall of one of the enemies of the church, here called Babylon, the prostitute or harlot. She represents everything anti-Christian in the world, everything that opposes Jesus. The form of

---

[1] Remember The Battle of Armageddon, like The Mark of the Beast is a description not a title. It refers to every battle in which believers are oppressed and God steps in to save. There have been many such adumbrations throughout history.

evil changes in time but the essence does not. It always contradicts God and the things of God.

The Revelation describes evil in the form of five enemies of Christ: the dragon, the beast out of the sea (persecuting governments), the beast out of the land (false teaching), Babylon, the harlot (seduction), and all men who wear the mark of the beast. The previous part discussed what happens to those who wear the mark of the beast. The bowls of wrath affect all men but especially evil. The final destruction (vv. 17–21) comes to those who oppose God while protecting the faithful. Now John sees the nature and demise of the dragon here called Babylon, the great prostitute.[1]

17:1–6

One of the seven angels invites John to see the judgment against Satan whom governments and nations worship. Their adulation of her is called adultery. Also they lead the world to swoon for her. She is presented sitting on a grotesque beast, probably the beast from out of the sea (13:1). This beast represents all governments that persecute the church. The woman of chapter 12 fled to the desert. The beast pursued her there. This women is dressed like a queen but she offers sinfulness to those who love her. These abominations include whatever might lure men away from faithful living, things that are evil in themselves as well as good things taken to extreme. Christians must be careful not to think of her as a friend. That leads dirtectly to thinking of God as the oppressor.

She has written on her forehead (possibly on a decorative band) her true identity. She is the source of all evil. She herself was drunk with blood-lust from persecuting the church. What John saw was too much. He wondered with great wonder. The double use of "wonder" is not merely redundant. It suggests that John was truly amazed.

We should not limit what Babylon represents. Like a jellyfish she has long and many tentacles. She uses industry, culture, commerce, sport, even leisure to entice men to evil. Luxury has a way of serving her ends. This is what John had called the cravings of sinful man, the

---

[1] It can be confusing that John switches from calling Satan the dragon to calling him the great prostitute. The emphasis is that as the great prostitute he tempts and lures men from faithfulness to Christ to wearing the mark of the beast.

lust of his eyes, and the boasting of what he has done.[1] She employs government persecution, cultural seduction, and false teaching in the church. In John's day this brought to mind Rome. In our day any government could be seen.

7:7–11

The angel explained the vision to John. The beast on which she rides was and is and will be. He is the antithesis of Jesus who was and is and is to come. Although God gained the upper hand, Satan will not quit so easily. He will rise up again as the time draws near, but this time he will face final judgment. The prostitute and the beast work together to persecute and seduce men. They scheme together how to lead men astray with false teaching. Together they function as an anti–Christian culture.

People whose names are not in the book of life wonder what it means that the beast is alive. The angel tries to make it clear. The seven heads represent the Seven Hills of Rome, the present beast. They also represent seven kings or kingdoms. Five have already had their turn, Assyria, Babylonia twice, Persia, and Greece. In all its forms the beast rose up after falling. A sixth king is Rome, and the seventh has not yet come. This probably represents every ensuing government that has chosen to harm the church. Paul wrote of a coming rebellion and the revealing of the man of lawlessness, doomed for destruction and who opposes God and exalts himself over God.[2]

17:12–14

The angel identifies the ten horns as every manifestation of anti–Christian behavior and thought. All will have power but for a limited time. And all will work with the beast to destroy the church. We see in this the crux of the vision, that Satan makes war against God. He will lose. Throughout the Christian age the church overcomes the opposition in whatever form. The anti–Christ may appear to be winning but his ruin is certain. Jesus is and always has been Lord of Lords and King of Kings. He stands victorious with His followers beside Him.

---

[1] 1 John 2:16
[2] 2 Thess 2:3ff

17:15–18

Apparently John saw some sort of pool representing the peoples and nations washing over the prostitute. They loved and worshiped her but now hate her. They will destroy all that she is because they recognize the error of their ways, but it's too late. The movement is like this: men loved her and joined her in adultery for what she offered in life. They continually hardened themselves against God until they became absolutely opposite God. When the judgment begins they suffer remorse but can do nothing to change. They will be punished alongside Babylon.

When the world tries to seduce us we should think about Jesus when the devil took Him to a very high mountain and showed Him all the kingdoms of the world and their splendor, All this I will give you. if you will bow down and worship me." Jesus said to him, Away from me, Satan! For it is written: "Worship the Lord your God, and serve him only."[1]

Chapter 18 is more description of the fall of Babylon (Satan), and it is ugly. Babylon represents all the evil (past, present, and future) and in this vision is treated as an individual. Her fall is announced as if it has already happened so certain is the coming destruction.

18:1-3

Another angel who is glorious to behold comes from Heaven with the authority to pronounce truth. He celebrates the fall of Babylon because she is reaping what she has sown. She is the embodiment of everything detestable and she has led men to join her in her sin. Men of influence and men who control the "things" of the earth enjoyed her promised pleasures without regard for eternity.

18:4–8

Another speaker from Heaven calls God's people out of the sins of Babylon or they too will suffer total destruction and punishment. God sees what all men do and think and will bring about retribution. She (and they) will experience intense grief. In her arrogance she thought she was mightier than God but she will be brought down,

---
[1] Matt 4:8–10

her glory gone.

Why is she falling so hard? It's because she and her lovers, governments, culture, and false teachers love the world and not God. Through all the ages of earth God has called men to flee the sins of Babylon and ignore her enticements. Whoever stays with her will experience the same fate. She will get back what she has coming equal to what she has done to God's people.

18:9–19

How terrible the judgment must be if those who sinned with her are traumatized when they see her fall. Men who control government and commerce will cry when they see how everything they love is gone. The power, the wealth, the luxury and pleasure they enjoyed will be suddenly worthless. Every category of valuable things will be gone. You can't take it with you. Not just the mighty and powerful but those of the working class will mourn for her and follow her in death for they too pursued the things of earth.

18:20

Team Jesus is invited to rejoice over the demise of Babylon the great. The question of 6:10, "How long must we wait?" Is answered. No longer!

18:21–24

The last four verses of this chapter emphasize the totality and finality of the judgment against Babylon. It is complete and irreversible. It will take great strength to carry out the promised destruction. It calls to mind the weight of the decision to send young men off to war. An angel strong enough to press a large mill stone will hurl it into the sea to demonstrate how Babylon will be hurled into hell. The stone is buried so far in the sea that it would never be recovered. Evil will be punished for eternity. Think what you will about hell, whether it is real or a metaphor, but according to this it will not be short. The world of luxury and pleasure that lured men away from God with the lusts of the flesh, culture that deceived men to choose another way than the way of God, and the teachers who perverted the truth will be punished eternally.

The judgment will mean that evil persons will never be found, they will never hear music again, light will never shine for them, and they will never hear the voice of the Bridegroom and His bride. Men of influence and power who completely ignored God and built themselves up with no regard for God and whose magic seduced many other men into sin will fall along with Babylon the great. The blood of persecuted believers will be on their account.

As we move to chapter 19 we see a celebration of righteousness. All of Heaven is rejoicing at the Christ's victory over evil.

19:1–8

We'll not comment on every symbol in this as we should have a good understanding of them by now. In Psalm–like fashion everyone in Heaven including the 24 Elders (representing the old and new covenant believers) and the four living creatures and the angels shout "Hallelujah!"[1] They sing of God's glory and power and the salvation He has won. They declare that what God did in saving the faithful and judging the wicked is just and fair.

The great prostitute/Babylon has earned her destiny for deceiving many and murdering others. The church is granted (not earned) a place at the wedding of the Lamb for her faithfulness. The bride (the church) is dressed in righteousness. Many images from ancient Jewish weddings come to mind. However, that is not necessary for our purpose here except to say that the bride is dressed appropriately and she has longed for this day. This wedding leads the bride into eternity in Heaven.

19:9–10

When the angel told John to write a beatitude to those who remained faithful to Christ, he feels compelled to worship the angel, like Paul in Lystra.[2] The angel rebuked his offering for he too is a created being. And worship belongs to God alone.

At this point Babylon has been vanquished. The vision turns to the beast and the false prophet and all who followed and worshiped them.

---

[1] This is the only use of hallelujah in the New Testament.
[2] Acts 14:11–15

19:11–16

For a second time John reports that Heaven was opened for him to look inside (4:1).[1] Christ appears on a white horse of victory and conquest. He is called faithful and true. This is Jesus at His second coming. He judges righteously because He is just and sees the very soul of men and angels. He wears wreaths of victory. He has a new name.[2]

His robe is dipped in the blood of His enemies. His name is "The Word of God" (John 1:1). He is not alone but accompanied by all the angels in Heaven. They too are dressed as victors. Out of His mouth is a sword to punish. He treads the winepress of God's wrath (14:18–20) carrying out the judgment of God. His name is identified also to be King of Kings and Lord of Lords. He is the ultimate champion.

19:17–21

The death of the beasts and their followers is so certain that an angel invites birds to feast on the flesh of their corpses. This is the ending of the Battle of Armageddon. The beast who rules the earth, and all his followers who wield power on earth are gathered as one to oppose Christ. It's Team Satan versus Team Jesus. This war was won when Jesus came, died, and rose again. The capture of the beast from the sea (13:1) and the beast from out of the land, the false prophet/teacher (13:11), leads to them being thrown into the eternal lake of fire prepared for Satan and his angels.[3] These are the leaders of the anti–Christian persecution, seduction, and false teaching.

I'll quote Hendriksen here, "The meaning is that at Christ's second coming Satan's persecution of the church and his power to deceive on earth shall cease forever. Every influence of Satan, whether in the direction of persecution or deception, goes with him to hell. Never again to appear anywhere outside of hell."[4]

---

[1] Peter had a similar experience recorded in Acts 10:11.
[2] In every use of "new name" in The Revelation it refers to God or Christ (3:12; 14:1; 22:4). See also 2:17.
[3] Matt 25:41
[4] Hendriksen, pg. 201

PART SEVEN: 20:1–22:21

We have finally come to the last and perhaps the most critical part of the vision. In these, the last three chapters we see the sequence of the plan of God. We see history in a new way. In chapter 19 we saw the final judgment, the end of history. Here in chapter 20 we return to the beginning of the millennium and the coming of Jesus to earth and immediately move to judgment day.

There are some interesting similarities between the movement from part three into part four as here from part six into part seven. Earlier in 11:18 the time for judgment has come and in12:5 Satan is hurled down from Heaven. In 19:20 the beast and the false prophet were cast into the fiery lake. In 20:2 Satan is seized and bound for 1000 years. In 12:5 Jesus is born and snatched up to God while Satan is hurled down from Heaven with limited power over men. In 20:3 again we see Satan thrown into the Abyss limiting his power. Thus the church is successful to evangelize.

In 11:3 the church was given the power to witness of Jesus for a time, and Satan was prevented from stopping her. This was not new information. Prior to the first coming of Christ the world was under the control of Satan, the prince of this world.[1] Satan did not have absolute power over men but was able to deceive and blind the minds of unbelievers so that they cannot see the light.[2] God had allowed people to choose their own way.[3] Everything changed when Jesus came and bound the Devil.[4] Here John saw that Satan had been bound for 1000 years, referring to the Christian age. We're in that 1000 year period now. There will not be 1000 years of man-made peace on earth prior to the second coming of Christ. The world will not get better without the cleansing power of Christ. Still the Gospel will be preached. Many will respond. Many will not.

Chapter 11 tells of a short time of intense persecution when

---

[1] John 12:31, 14:30, 16:11

[2] 2 Cor 4:4

[3] Acts 14:16

[4] It is interesting to note that after Jesus healed a demon-possessed man the Pharisees concluded that it was by the power of the prince of demons that He drives out demons. Jesus' response was to point out that He could do this because Satan had been bound, how can anyone enter a strong man's house and carry off his possessions unless he first ties up the strong man? Then he can rob his house. Matt 12:29. The phrase "ties up" is the same word "bound" used in Rev 20:2. Being bound Satan cannot stop the church from witnessing of Christ and proclaiming the truth to all nations. It remains true however that many will still not believe God, refusing to accept Him in spite of His judgments against evil in the present age. They will harden their hearts.

Satan is released. Chapter 20 also references this short time of persecution describing the Battle of Armageddon. The severe persecution is followed by the Second Coming of Christ and judgment. In the words of A.W. Tozer, the world is not a playground. It's a battlefield.

Our fallen culture seems beautiful, attractive and pleasing. Revelation exposes it as ugly, off–putting, and deceitful. The world is a prostitute chasing every religion and philosophy. She will be destroyed.

20:1–3

An angel in the service of God's plan seizes Satan and throws him into the Abyss. I find it interesting that the Abyss has a shaft with a lid that is sealable and lockable. The timetable as we have seen is not ten centuries but a long time when the church is free to preach about Jesus. Satan cannot stop or destroy the church but he can disrupt the Gospel age. I don't know why God chose to allow Satan a short time of freedom before he is judged, but the vision clearly says He does.

We next see the victorious church.

20:4–6

The people who read this book in John's day most surely had seen Christians murdered in brutal and vicious ways because they would not bow to Caesar. Despite the severity of the persecution many remained faithful to Jesus. To encourage the readers the vision includes images of souls of murdered believers who had died in Christ, now reigning with Jesus. They have won their part of the battle. These souls are finished with earth. They are enjoying the first resurrection, free from the second death.

20:7–10

In the short time that Satan is released he will gather all of his "friends" to fight in the battle against Christ and oppress the church. The mention of Gog and Magog is from Ezekiel where he spoke of Syria under Antiochus Epiphanes who mercilessly slaughtered Israel. John used this typology to create a picture of Satan's attack on believers.

The four corners of the earth refers to the whole earth. He's not speaking of a military battle with nations united against nations. It's not a prediction of specific 21st century nations at war. This is again the Battle of Armageddon. Unlike other visions of the battle, in this one we see what happens to Satan in the end.

It's helpful for us to realize that there will not be a new warning that the destruction of evil is about to happen. It will be sudden and unexpected. Some of Team Satan, the beasts and the false prophet had already been thrown into the lake of fire. Now Satan too is hurled into the everlasting torment.

The remainder of this chapter presents a powerful picture of the judgment.

20:11–15

John sees Jesus on His throne.[1] The Earth and sky running from His presence is not about destruction but about renewal for the creation itself will be liberated from its bondage to decay and brought into the glorious freedom of the children of God.[2] Jesus said that at the renewal of all things, the Son of Man will be seated on His glorious throne. In his sermon in Acts 3, Peter declared that when the time comes for God to restore everything to His original creation, Jesus will come from Heaven, just as God promised.[3] In his second epistle he wrote of the earth and sky, The day of the Lord will come like a thief. The heavens will disappear with a roar, the elements will be destroyed by fire, and the earth and everything in it will be laid bare.[4]

At this time everyone stands before the throne. Books are opened, presumably a book of each person's life and the Book of Life. Each man is judged according to his own works. For a believer there is no record of sin because sins were forgiven by Jesus.

Death and Hades give up their dead. Death is the separation of the soul from the body. Hades is the state of being so separated. Death no longer exists and Hades is unnecessary so they too are

---

[1] When the Son of Man comes in His glory, and all the angels with Him, He will sit on His throne in heavenly glory. Matt 25:31
[2] Rom 8:21
[3] Acts 3:21
[4] 2 Pet 3:10

thrown into the lake of fire, the second death.

It's clear from this text that hell (an eternal lake of fire and torment) is real. Satan and his agents and angels will be thrown into it. So also will be all whose names are not written in the book of life. The judgment is serious business.

We will offer limited comment on the last two chapters as the message is clear enough on its own. We also will not try to find meaning in the mention of specific jewels and ornaments mentioned in describing the new Jerusalem. The descriptions are intended to create a beautiful setting for an eternal personal relationship with God/Jesus.

21:1–4

God had created a perfect world that was damaged by sin. All of creation was affected by man's sin but now is restored to its original splendor. Every ugly evil thing is destroyed or changed. No longer will we see the scars left by sin. The curses of Genesis 3 are undone. Men who believe God and remain faithful now experience the personal presence of God. This is the fulfillment of God's promise to be our God and we His people.

21:5–8

Jesus declared that His words are true and trustworthy. As this vision has been about encouraging and warning believers to resist persecution, cultural seduction, and false teaching, the reward is given to the overcomers. We wear the seal of God and His name. In contrast, the cowardly who surrendered to the oppression and deceit of the evil one, who did not believe God, who did not accept Him as God, the fiery lake prepared for Satan is their self–chosen destiny.

21:9–22:6

This is a vision, and what a vision it is. A holy city of faithful believers, conquerors, the elect. True Israel. The structure, the walls, and adornments symbolize perfection and beauty. The church is now in perfect unity with God. This is the bride of the Lamb. High walls suggest protection and safety from evil as well as security in fellowship with God. Only those whose names are written in the

Book of Life may enter.

It is built on the names of the tribes of Israel and the Apostles of Christ. The images are beautiful and difficult to describe with words. The city is bedazzled with jewels, pearls, and gold. There is no temple (no need, God is present), no light (no need, God is light), gates are always open, and a river of life flows from the throne of God. This is total abundant life. This is the truth. This is what the Lord wanted John to see and write about (1:1, 22:6).

22:7–9

As John's incredible vision closes he quotes Jesus and adds his own testimony, Behold, I am coming soon! John attests that he was an eyewitness to this experience. For a second time he falls to his knees in worship but the angel stops him (19:10).

22:10–11

John is told to not seal the words of this prophecy. In the timeline of history, the end is near. God is saying that He has given free will to choose Him (Team Jesus) or evil (Team Satan). Whatever you choose, so be it. He will get out of your way. Now it's too late to change. There is no more chance to repent. Everyone receives what reward or punishment is due.

22:12–16

This is Jesus' final encouragement to long–suffering believers. Again we hear the distinction between believers (Team Jesus) and those who reject Jesus (Team Satan). This is Jesus' final beatitude. Those who are washed in the blood of Jesus are promised access to the Tree of Life. Jesus Himself testifies that these words are true and faithful based on the reality of who He is, the promised Messiah.

22:17–21

The first "come" may be calling the entire plan of God as described in this vision to come to being, including the curses, the plagues, the destruction, the punishment for evil and the promise of life for the church. The second "come" invites those who wear the name of Christ, who have been faithful to the end to come into His eternal presence and to be completely fulfilled. It is an invitation to the wedding of Christ to His bride.

Because this vision is true and meant for all people of all ages no one should dare take away from it or change it by adding something new. To do so would be to surrender a place in the Heaven.

John is not the author of The Revelation, Jesus is. Jesus says, I am coming soon! John agrees and says, Yes! Come Lord Jesus! This preacher too says, "Come Lord Jesus!"

READER'S STUDY GUIDE

I encourage the reader to use this guide to help you remember the points made at the beginning of this book. Answering these questions in your own words will help you as you read through the comments on the text of The Revelation.

What is the purpose of The Revelation?

Describe the context of John's vision.

Briefly define the techniques used in writing The Revelation.
- Repetition
- Recapitulation
- Symbols
- Typology
- Hyperbole
- Progressive Parallelism

What are the four ways the word "heaven" is used in the Bible?

What is the Kingdom of God?

What is the Millennium?

Who or what is true Israel in the Revelation?

What is the Battle of Armageddon?

What does "The Great Tribulation" describe?

What four things can we know for certain about the Second Coming of Christ?

What are the five realities we can know about life after death?

What is the Rapture and where does this idea come from?

What do we know about judgment?

APPENDIX

Francis Chan made this challenging list concerning "lukewarm" Christians:

1. Lukewarm people attend church fairly regularly. It's what is expected of them, what they believe "good Christians" do, so they attend.

2. Lukewarm people give money to charity and to the church as long as it doesn't impinge on their standard of living. If they have a little extra and it's easy and safe to give, they do so.

3. Lukewarm people choose what is popular over what is right when they are in conflict. They desire to fit in both at church and outside of church; they care more about what people think of them than what God thinks of their hearts.

4. Lukewarm people don't really want to be saved from their sin; they want only to be saved from the penalty of their sin.

5. Lukewarm people are moved by stories of people who do radical things for Christ, yet they don't act themselves. They assume such action is for "extreme" Christians, not average ones.

6. Lukewarm people rarely share their faith with their neighbors, coworkers, or friends. They don't want to be rejected.

7. Lukewarm people gauge their morality or "goodness" by comparing themselves to the secular world. They feel satisfied that while they aren't as hard-core for Jesus as so-and-so, they are nowhere as horrible as the guy down the street.

8. Lukewarm people say they love Jesus, and He is a part of their lives, their money, and their thoughts, but He isn't allowed to control their lives.

9. Lukewarm people love God, but they don't love Him all with all their heart, soul, and strength.

10. Lukewarm people love others but not as much as they love themselves. Their love for others is typically focused on those who love them in return. There is little love left over for those who cannot

love them back, much less for those who intentionally slight them, or with whom conversations are awkward or uncomfortable.

11. Lukewarm people will serve God and others, but there are limits to how far they will go or how much time, money, and energy they're willing to give.

12. Lukewarm people think about life on earth much more often than eternity.

13. Lukewarm people are thankful for their luxuries and comforts, and rarely consider trying to give to the poor.

14. Lukewarm people do whatever is necessary to keep themselves from feeling too guilty. They want to do the bare minimum, to be "good enough" without requiring too much of them.

15. Lukewarm people play it safe. This focus on safe living keeps them from sacrificing and risking for God.

16. Lukewarm people feel secure because they attend church, made a profession of faith at age twelve, were baptized, come from a Christian family, vote Republican, or live in America.

17. Lukewarm people do not live by faith. They don't need God to help them. They don't genuinely seek out what life God would have them live, they have life figured out. They don't depend on God on a daily basis because their refrigerators are full and, for the most part, they are in good health. The truth is, their lives wouldn't look much different if they suddenly stopped believing in God.

18. Lukewarm people drink and swear less than average, but besides that, they really aren't very different from a typical unbeliever. They equate their partially sanitized lives with holiness.

If you just saw yourself, I pray that God has turned up the heat today. Do not ignore the Word of God. Repent and obey. This was very serious when John wrote it and it's very serious today.

BIBLIOGRAPHY

Barclay, William, *Revelation Vol.1*, Westminster Press, Philadelphia, 1960.

Bonhoeffer, Dietrich, *Life Together*, HarperOne, 1978.

Caird, C.B., *The Revelation of St. John the Divine*, Black's New Testament Commentary, Peabody, MA, 1966

Campbell, Clive, *Messiah: 2020*.

Cottrell, Jack, *Bible Prophecy and End Times*, A Twelve–Part Sermon Series on CD, College Press, Joplin, 2006.

Hendriksen, William, *More Than Conquerors*, Baker Books, 2015.

Lindsey, Hal, *The Late Great Planet Earth*, Zondervan, 1970

Lowery, Robert, *Revelation's Rhapsody*, College Press, Joplin, 2006.

Morris, Leon, Tyndale New Testament Commentaries, *The Gospel According to Luke*, Eerdmans, Grand Rapids, 1974.

North American Christian Convention 2013, Sermons: *Love the Church Honestly*, Aaron Brockett; *Worship God Selflessly*, Randy Harris; *Endure Suffering Patiently*, Jon Weece; *See Evil Clearly*, Kyle Idleman; *Welcome Salvation Joyfully*, Rick Atchley; *Encounter Christ Powerfully*, Matt Proctor.

Proctor, Matt, *Victorious, A Devotional Study Guide*, College Press, Joplin, 2013.

Websters New Ideal Dictionary, Springfield, MA, G. & C. Merriam Company, 1973.

www.ingramcontent.com/pod-product-compliance
Lightning Source LLC
Chambersburg PA
CBHW070334180426
43196CB00050B/2630